THE ANTIPODEANS

challenge and response
in Australian art 1955–1965

■ national gallery of **australia**

Produced by the Publications Department
of the National Gallery of Australia, Canberra

Editor: Pauline Green
Designer: Kirsty Morrison
Photography: Richard Pedvin and Eleni Kypridis
Prepress: ColourboxDigital, Perth, WA
Printed in Australia by Lamb Print, Perth, WA

Cataloguing-in-Publication data
The Antipodeans: challenge and response in Australian art
1955–1965
Bibliography.
ISBN 0 642 54158 2.
1. Art, Abstract – Australia – Exhibitions. 2. Figurative art –
Australia – Exhibitions. 3. Art, Australian – Exhibitions.
I. National Gallery of Australia.
709.94074

Distributed in Australia by:
Thames and Hudson
11 Central Boulevard Business Park, Port Melbourne,
Victoria 3207

Distributed in the United Kingdom by:
Thames and Hudson
30–34 Bloomsbury Street, London WC1B 3QP

Distributed in the United States of America by:
University of Washington Press
1326 Fifth Avenue, Ste. 555, Seattle, WA 98101-2604

(front cover) **John Olsen** *Bush walk* 1957 (detail)

(back cover) **John Perceval** *Fighting angels* 1959

THE ANTIPODEANS: CHALLENGE AND RESPONSE
IN AUSTRALIAN ART 1955–1965

An exhibition at the National Gallery of Australia, Canberra
27 November 1999 – 5 March 2000

Curator: Deborah Clark, Assistant Curator of Australian
Paintings and Sculptures, National Gallery of Australia
Research Assistant: Steve Tonkin

The selection of artists and works of art included in
the exhibition was largely determined by the collection
of the National Gallery of Australia. The absence of work
by some significant artists of the period indicates only that the
most appropriate works are not held by the National Gallery.
In all, thirty-three artists are represented in the exhibition,
including the seven Antipodeans.

ACKNOWLEDGEMENTS

I would like to thank Elizabeth Summons, Kerry Stokes, and
Janet Holmes à Court, who have generously made available
works for loan. I am especially grateful to Elizabeth Summons,
Robert Dickerson, David Boyd, Charles Blackman, Bernard
Smith, Helen Brack, and Christopher Heathcote, who willingly
gave their time to talk to me; their insights into the period were
of great value.

I thank Brian Kennedy, Director, National Gallery of Australia,
and Ron Ramsey, General Manager, Access Services, who
supported the exhibition from its inception; and John McDonald
who encouraged its progress when he had only just come in
to head the Australian Art Department.

I owe a special debt of gratitude to Steve Tonkin who has been
an able and enthusiastic Research Assistant, who has worked
tirelessly on all aspects of the exhibition as well as contributing
an essay for the catalogue. I was fortunate to have the research
skills of Greg Evans, who prepared the bibliography for the
catalogue. I thank my professional colleagues for their
assistance, particularly Diane Johnson, Administrative Assistant
in the Australian Art Department, whose efforts on behalf of the
exhibition have been considerable. And thanks, as always,
to Tim Fisher for his advice and encouragement on this
exhibition, the latest chapter in a continuing conversation
about art.

The production of the catalogue is due to the efforts of
Pauline Green, editor, Kirsty Morrison, designer and
Suzie Campbell, Publications Manager. Thanks also to
Richard Pedvin and Eleni Kypridis who photographed the
works; and to Allan Byrne, Kim Brunoro, Sheridan Roberts,
Susie Bioletti, Andrea Wise, Beata Tworek-Matuszkiewicz
and Brian Cropp, who renewed many works for this exhibition.

Deborah Clark

CONTENTS

INTRODUCTION

By the time 'The Antipodean Manifesto' announced that 'the great Tachiste Emperor has no clothes', the line had already become one of the abiding clichés of modern art. No jeremiad against decadent, modernistic experimentation was complete without this ritual incantation, and so it remains to this day. It suggests that the objects of one's scorn are muddled, superficial fashion-victims, prepared to deceive an audience — and perhaps themselves. Not only is this a matter of deception and self-delusion, there are also the most alarming dangers: the rejection of life, the denial of tradition, and finally 'the death of art'.

It sounds strident and hysterical today, when movements have splintered into a thousand styles and subcultures. Yet it must be remembered that 1959 was the height of the Cold War, a time when Australia was beginning to take its cultural leads from America rather than Britain. This process would accelerate throughout the 1960s, until — by the end of the decade — New York, not London, was the destination of choice for young Australian artists who travelled overseas. Perhaps Bernard Smith and his colleagues could see it all coming. In the Manifesto, it is the emptying-out of humanistic values that most concerns the writers. They worry about a vanguard art that has become obsessed with abstract decoration at the expense of recognisable signs and symbols. It is an art that makes great claims for its own spiritual depths, but threatens to alienate a broad cross-section of the public; it is a self-consciously 'radical' art that has little time for politics.

How easy it is to forget that the artists such as Arthur Boyd and John Perceval had been considered radical artists themselves in the 1940s. As part of the group associated with the patrons, John and Sunday Reed, and the magazine, *Angry Penguins*,

Boyd and Perceval had been exponents of the most innovative expressionist painting this country had seen. The difference was that this work had been humanist in its inspiration, relying on strong, iconic images to make an impact. By contrast, the new abstract artists dealt in grand generalisations, in nuances and allusions. It was an art that sought to divorce feeling from figuration, allowing emotions to take on a tragic nobility. Such a work may have been 'only a blot' to the Antipodeans, but the abstractionists had the highest ambitions for their work.

What this confrontation announces is that modernism had finally taken charge of the Australian art scene, after many faltering attempts and false starts. The clash between figurative and abstract artists was enacted entirely within the confines of the avant-garde. Conventional Australian painting — with its gum trees and billabongs, its stately portraits and decorative still lifes — was largely indifferent to the claims of both parties. Suddenly the gum tree painters were no longer the enemy, they were simply irrelevant.

It is also worth noting that the dividing lines were not drawn up as strictly as the Manifesto would suggest. It seems absurd that an artist such as Fred Williams was omitted from the original Antipodeans group because it was felt that his art was too abstract. Neither was it true that Sydney fell largely into the abstract camp, while Melbourne was predominantly figurative. There was a high-profile group of figurative painters based in Sydney, including Russell Drysdale, William Dobell, Justin O'Brien and Jeffrey Smart. In Melbourne during these years, as Christopher Heathcote shows in his book, *A Quiet Revolution*, there was a flourishing school of abstract artists that included Leonard French, Roger Kemp, Ian and Dawn Sime.

History records that most of the artists associated with 'The Antipodean Manifesto' soon sought to distance themselves from the affair. The tone had been too hectoring for comfort, the oppositions too cut-and-dried. Instead of being defenders of the image, the Antipodeans began to look like cultural isolationists, intent on resisting the invasion of foreign influences. While this would never have been their underlying intention, in the progressive atmosphere of the 1960s any movement that spoke up in the name of tradition risked being stigmatised as an organ of the establishment.

After forty years we may look back and recognise that the Antipodean message was not merely reactionary or misguided, no matter how strident its tone. The same dilemmas are being perpetually re-enacted in the field of contemporary art, in the war between tradition and fashion. If we do not discern such a clear distinction between abstract and figurative art, it is because the triumph of abstraction has seen it become an everyday part of the vocabulary of art. The distinction has been absorbed and neutralised in much the same way as the once-militant division between Romantic and Neo-classical art. At the end of the century both the Antipodeans and their abstract antagonists have taken on the status of classics.

John McDonald

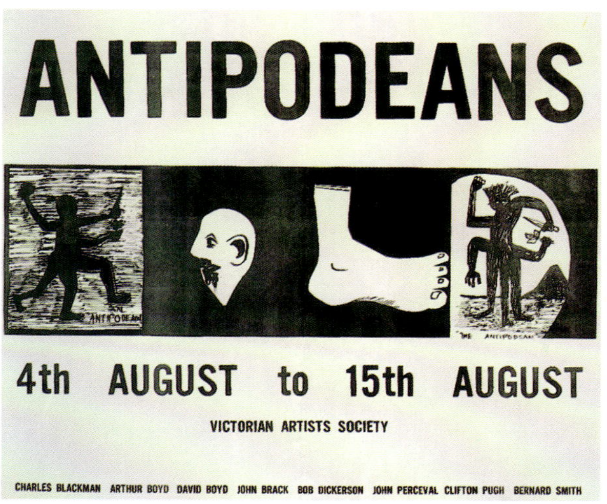

Charles Blackman *Antipodeans exhibition poster* 1959 lithograph 35.6 x 43.1 cm Gift of James Mollison 1985

IN DEFENCE OF THE IMAGE

In 1959 in Melbourne, seven artists and an art historian came together 'to defend and to champion … the place of the image in art'.[1] The group comprised Charles Blackman, Arthur Boyd, David Boyd, John Brack, John Perceval, Clifton Pugh and Robert Dickerson, who, as the 'Antipodeans', held just one exhibition together at the Victorian Artists' Society in August 1959. The art historian, Bernard Smith, the only non-painter of the group, drafted 'The Antipodean Manifesto' which accompanied the exhibition.

The event that has attained almost legendary status within the story of Australian art[2] had its beginnings in casual discussions amongst friends and fellow artists. The first official meeting of the group was held in February 1959. All those present were living in and around Melbourne and had been active members of the Contemporary Art Society during the late 1950s. Most of them had established local reputations; Clifton Pugh, Charles Blackman, John Perceval and Arthur Boyd had recently been included in the third *Survey* exhibition of contemporary art at the National Gallery of Victoria. Other possible members were suggested at that first meeting,[3] but the only one invited to join the group was the Sydney painter, Robert Dickerson.

Bernard Smith had suggested that they should call themselves Antipodeans — a name that would, avoid the nationalistic overtones of 'Australian' yet define the group's *place* in an international context.[4] As one contemporary reviewer explained: 'Antipodean means, by definition, to be diametrically the opposite of something.'[5] The name encapsulates Smith's aspirations for the group: that, both locally and in London, they should engage in a contemporary critique of European modernism. Prior to the formation

of the Antipodeans only Smith and David Boyd had travelled overseas, and it appears that a considerable incentive for the group was the prospect of an Antipodeans exhibition in London.[6] Their plans were overtaken however by the major survey exhibition of figurative and non-figurative painting, *Recent Australian Painting*, held at the Whitechapel Art Gallery, London, in 1961. Although all the Antipodeans were represented in this exhibition, their goal to take a small cohesive group show to London was never realised.

To accompany their Melbourne exhibition the artists felt that there should be a written statement outlining their views on art. John Brack, David Boyd, Clifton Pugh and Charles Blackman submitted 'artist's statements' for inclusion in the proposed document. Bernard Smith compiled the text as his 'special contribution to the show'.[7] The published declaration of principles, 'The Antipodean Manifesto', was the first of its kind in the history of Australian art. It is both the defining feature and the most problematic aspect of the group. It is a document from which the artists have generally distanced themselves in the years since the exhibition.

'The Antipodean Manifesto' was prominently placed in the exhibition catalogue preceding the list of works by the seven artists. In its final form the Manifesto leapt to the defence of the image, 'the recognisable shape, the meaningful symbol … fashioned by the artist from his perceptions and imaginative experience', and its 'capacity to refer to experiences the artist shares with his audience'. Although claiming not to advocate the creation of a 'national style', the Manifesto stated that it was both a right and the duty of the Australian artist to draw upon their 'experience both of society and nature in Australia for the materials' of their art.[8]

Since the time of its public exposure at the opening of the exhibition, 'The Antipodean Manifesto' has been scrutinised by commentators. Barbara Blackman later observed that the Manifesto became 'the evidence *in absentia*' by which the artists were judged.[9] Compounding this situation is the fact that many of the circumstances surrounding the group meetings and details of the formulation of the Manifesto only came to light some three decades after the event.[10] In the transition from private discussions to public forum the intentions of the artists in contributing to the Manifesto have been inadvertently lost.

The critical response to the exhibition was mixed. Arnold Shore, in the *Age*, commented: 'It is a pity that the ideas represented are often obscure, sometimes suggestive of comic-strip art or simply badly painted!' Supportive reviews were published in the newly established *Modern Art News* and in the *Nation*. Franz Philipp, a colleague of Bernard Smith at the University of Melbourne, claimed in the *Nation* that no-one who had seen 'fashionable and trite non-figuration … will deny sympathy to the manifesto's assertion of the communicative nature of art'. Alan McCulloch in the *Herald*, under the heading 'Battle Cry of Antipodeans', suggested the show was 'a call to arms to modern figurative painters to save art from the inroads of non-figuration'. His review the following week began, 'Figurative — or abstract? — it's a big decision for an artist today'.[11]

The Antipodeans exhibition has entered the story of Australian art as championing figurative modernism, just as the *Direction 1* exhibition in Sydney in 1956 is viewed as a crystallising event in the story of abstraction in Australia. Both exhibitions are perceived as defining points of rivalry between figurative and non-figurative art in Australia in the 1950s. Most significant in establishing this perception was Bernard Smith's *Australian Painting 1788–1960*, published in 1962, in which the 'theatrical extravaganza' of the Antipodeans' defence of the 'image' against abstraction is presented as the culminating event in Australian art to 1960.[12]

The notion that abstraction dominated art in Sydney and figuration in Melbourne is a somewhat distorted view. If there were differences in artistic practice between Sydney and Melbourne it was a reflection of differences in the intellectual climate and social networks in these cities rather than a divide based on merely formal concerns. There were a number of important essentially non-figurative artists resident in Melbourne, such as Roger Kemp, Leonard French, Ian Sime, and Grahame and Inge King; and the aggressively avant-garde Gallery A had opened in Melbourne two weeks before the Antipodeans exhibition. Gallery A became a focal point for exhibiting non-figurative art in Australia and was the venue for the *Nine Sydney Artists* exhibition in 1961,[13] which has since been portrayed as Sydney's 'official' response to the Antipodeans.

While the Antipodeans' defence of the 'image' against abstraction has become an almost legendary episode in the history of Australian painting, the staging of this 'counter-revolution' does not fully reflect the complexity of the art scene of the late 1950s. However, the Antipodean intervention did bring together a number of prominent modernist painters. At that time, Charles Blackman, Arthur Boyd, David Boyd, John Brack, Robert Dickerson, John Perceval and Clifton Pugh were all creating work of lasting significance to Australian art.

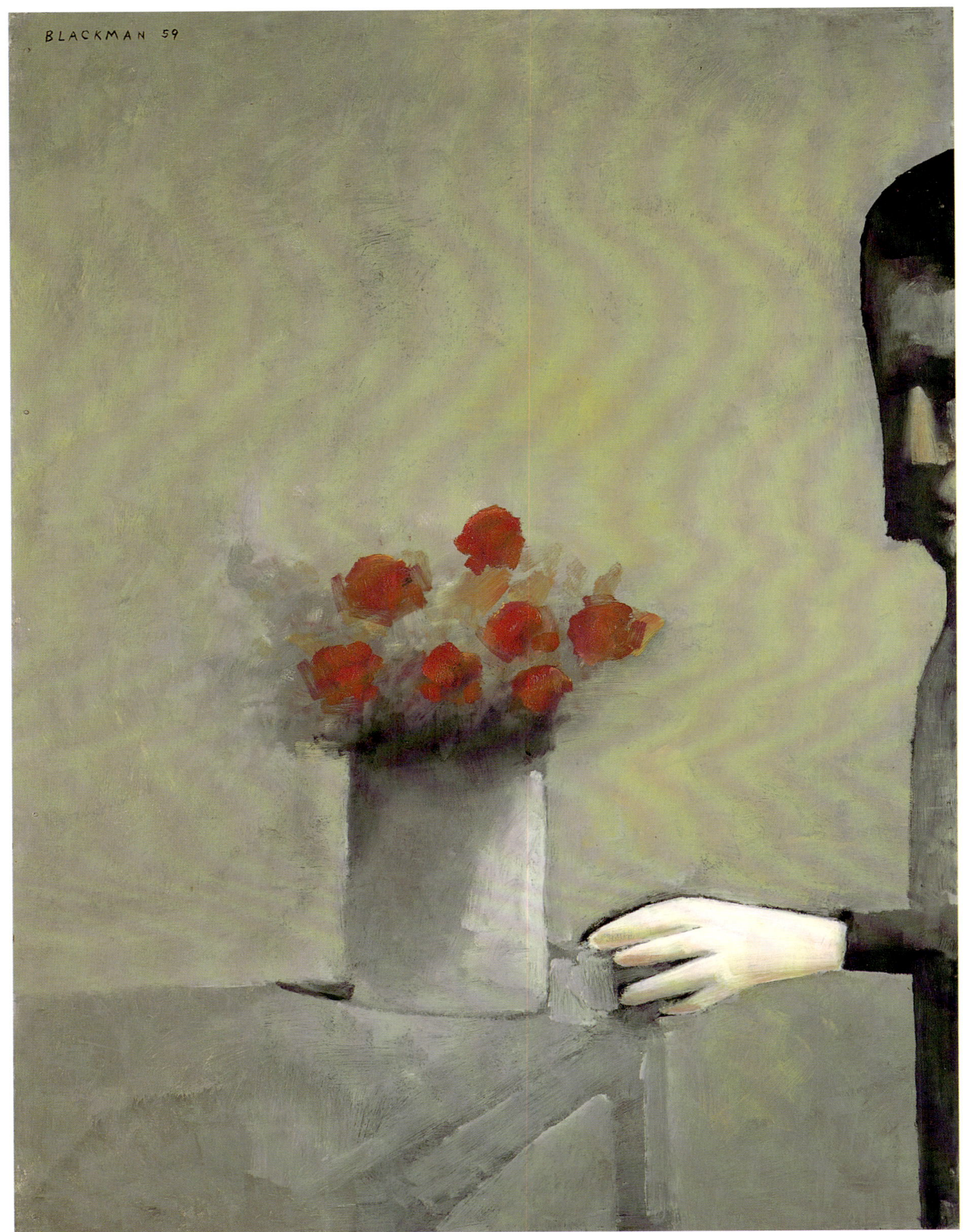
BLACKMAN 59

Charles Blackman had been drawn to the creative atmosphere of Melbourne in the early 1950s. Childhood innocence and vulnerability are constant themes in his work, as in *Schoolgirl* and *Fleeing schoolgirl*, both of 1953. In the late 1950s his work softened to focus on inner moods and feelings through a synthesis of figures and flowers. These paintings search for a delicate balance between detachment from, and engagement with, the viewer.

In *Silence* 1959, the luminous vase of flowers dominates the centre of the picture, with the shadowy silhouette of a girl hidden at the edge of the frame. It appears that Blackman is struggling to find a compositional variation on the central figure clutching a bouquet of flowers. In this work the flowers do not so much reflect the inner world of the girl, but provide the antithetical indication of her feelings, heightened by the physical separation of flowers and figure. For Blackman the work may have a personal reference, to the onset of his wife's blindness. While the flowers shout with luminosity, the separation of the vase from the touch of the girl with her obscured eyes and face suggests the visual beauty of the flowers cannot be experienced.

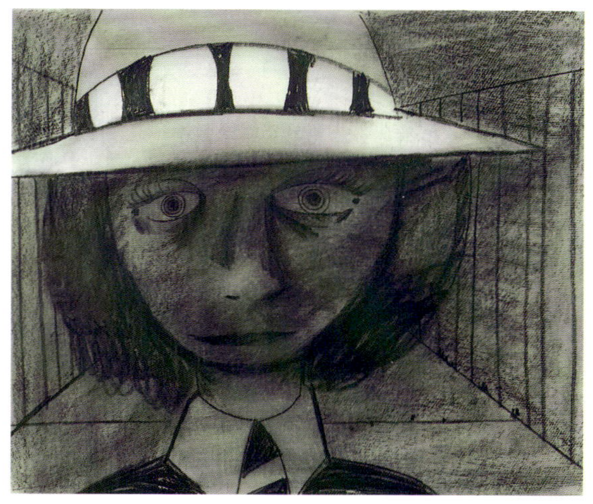

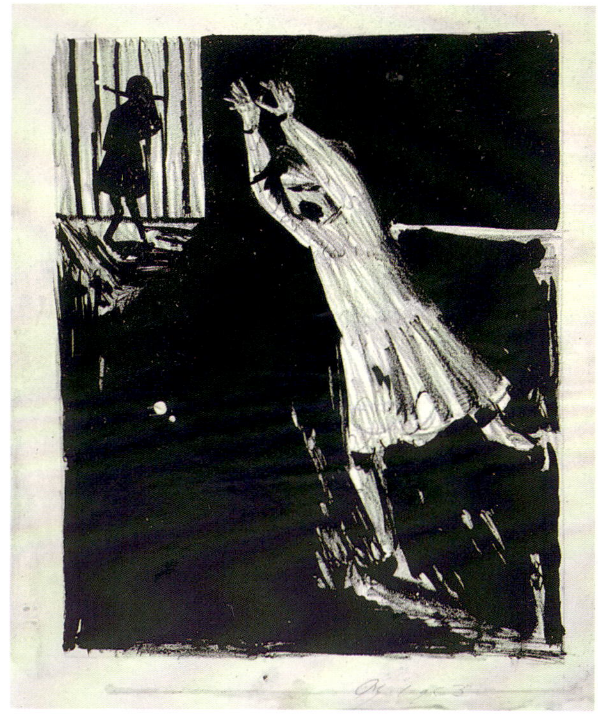

(opposite page) **Charles Blackman** *Silence* 1959 oil on composition board 121.0 x 91.0 cm
(this page above) *Schoolgirl* 1953 charcoal on paper 61.0 x 76.0 cm
(below) *Fleeing schoolgirl* 1953 lithograph 26.0 x 20.4 cm

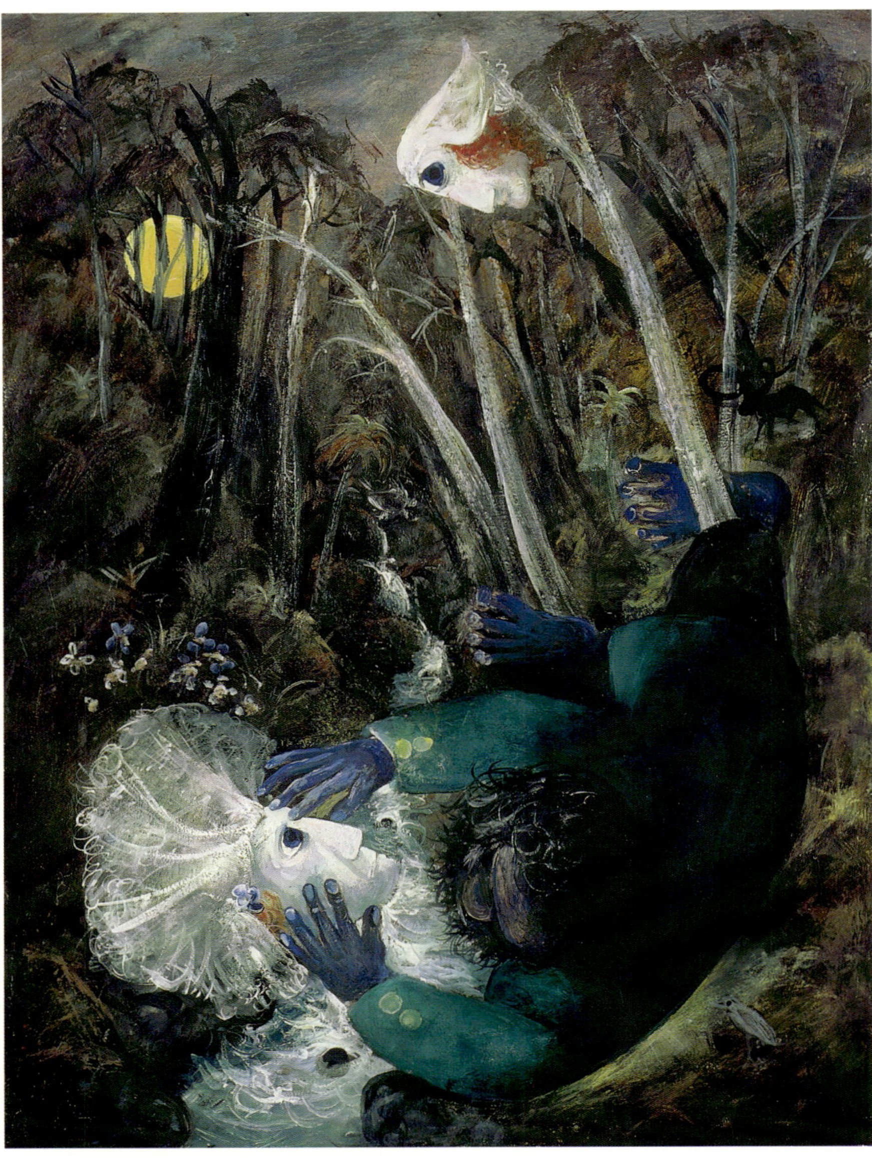

Arthur Boyd was deeply affected by a trip to central Australia in 1951 where he witnessed at first hand the appalling conditions imposed upon Aboriginal communities. Boyd recorded the trip in his sketchbooks and from these drawings painted his *Love, Marriage and Death of a Half-caste* series 1957–59 in which he uses marriage as a metaphor to examine universal themes of displacement and separation.

An important painting from the series, *Reflected bride I* 1958,[14] presents the hopelessness of the situation as a narcissistic obsession with the unattainable. Franz Philipp, in his major monograph on Arthur Boyd, claimed that this series made a greater impact on the public than any work of the artist's preceding it, and represented a turning point in Boyd's life and in his artistic career.[15]

Arthur Boyd *Reflected bride I* 1958 oil and tempera on composition board 122.0 x 90.0 cm
Reproduced with permission of Bundanon Trust

In the late 1950s, David Boyd returned to painting after a decade concentrating on commercial pottery, for which his skills were widely admired. In the Antipodeans exhibition he showed paintings from his recent *Tasmanians* series, based on the fate of the Tasmanian Aborigines after white settlement. *Truganini — a dream of childhood* 1958–59 is a major work from the series.

David Boyd's commitment to confronting issues of injustice is highlighted in his statement submitted to Bernard Smith for inclusion in 'The Antipodean Manifesto': 'I believe the artist to be a kind of moralist … By "moralist" I mean the artist's function to continually remind the community of the need to adhere to human values …'[16]

While both Arthur Boyd's *Reflected bride I* and David Boyd's *Truganini — a dream of childhood* allude to universal moral issues, the latter work is directly tied to the Australian context by its specific subject matter. It is David Boyd's personal response to the fate of Truganini (Trukanini), the so-called 'last Tasmanian', and the trials of her childhood.

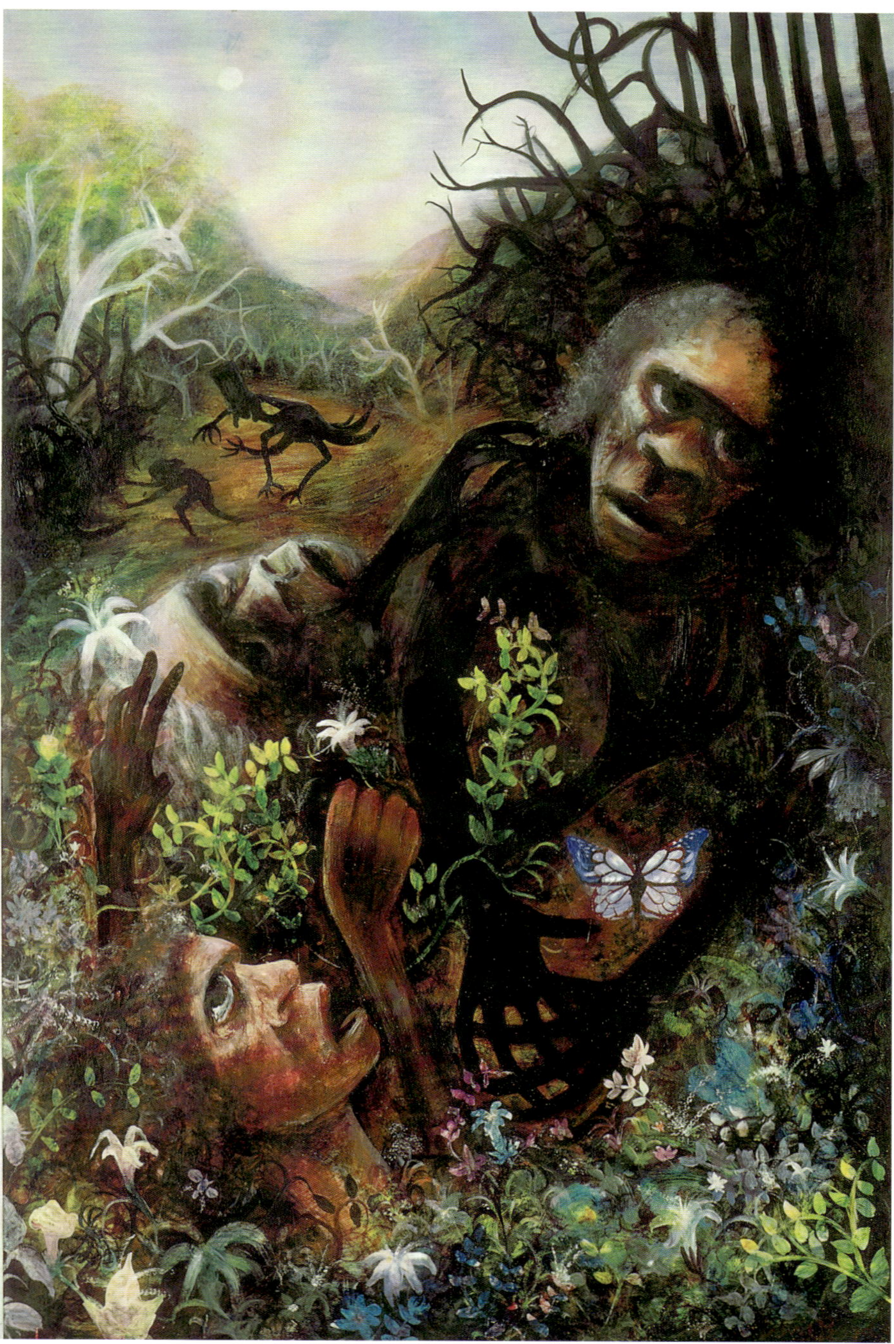

David Boyd *Truganini — a dream of childhood* 1958–59 oil on composition board
181.5 x 119.5 cm

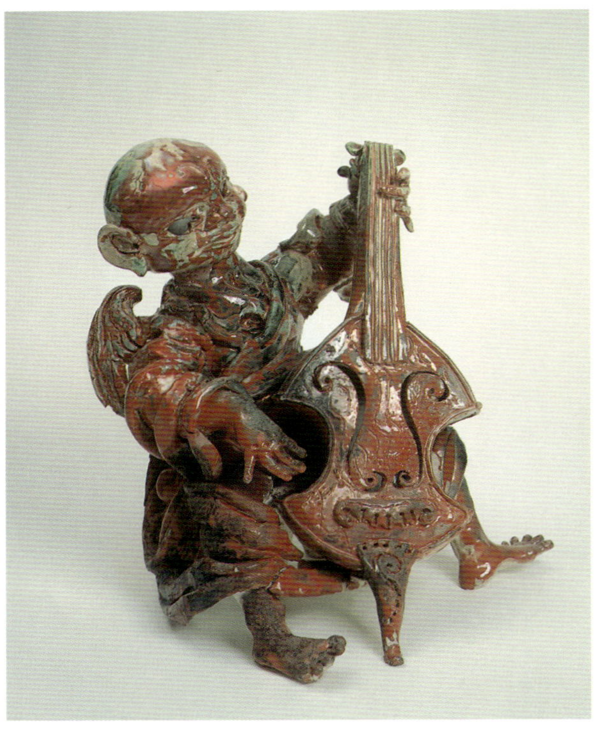

John Perceval was the only member of the group to include sculptural work in the Antipodeans exhibition. He had first shown his angels at the Museum of Modern Art in Melbourne in 1958. 'In these works he has attained a pitch of technical excellence unrivalled by any other ceramic sculptor in Australia', claimed Alan McCulloch in the *Herald*.[17] Perceval achieved a personal breakthrough with the *sang-de-boeuf* glaze (the name denotes the ox-blood red colour of the glaze) which gives his figures a dramatic tension between the angelic and mischievous, human and the divine.

Perceval had returned to painting in the mid-1950s with his *Williamstown* and *Gaffney's Creek* paintings, and in 1960 was a joint winner of the Wynne Prize for landscape at the Art Gallery of New South Wales. His work of the period is characterised by the fluid confident use of materials, reflecting a fusion of conception and execution in an intuitive response to the subject. *Black Tasmanian Wattle* 1960 was exhibited in *Antipodean Vision*, the officially sponsored exhibition of Australian painting held at the Tate Gallery in London in 1963. The expressive impasto surface of the foliage, while appearing spontaneously executed, is stabilised by the underlying structure of the black limbs of the wattle. In his landscapes of the early 1960s, the physical gesture of painting, animated colours and texture of the paint increasingly consume the transcription of the subject matter.[18]

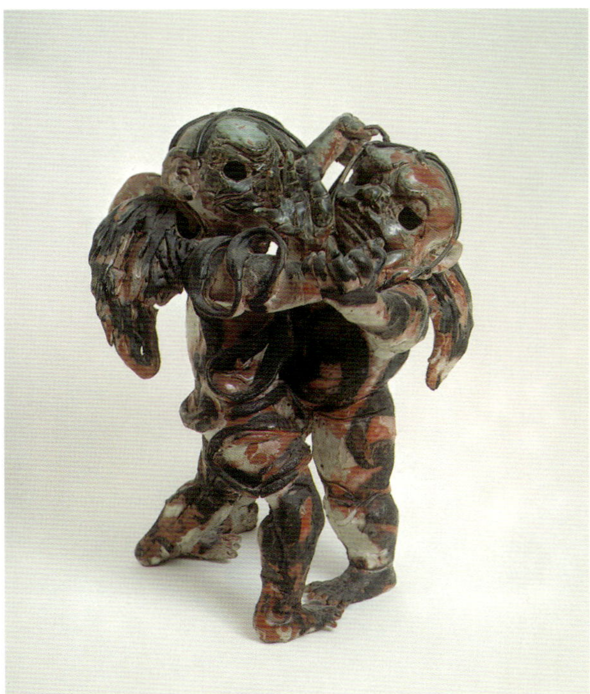

(this page above) **John Perceval** *Angel playing a cello* 1957 earthenware height 30.3 cm
(below) *Fighting angels* 1959 earthenware height 36.7 cm
(opposite page) *Black Tasmanian Wattle* 1960 oil on canvas on composition board 83.7 x 91.3 cm

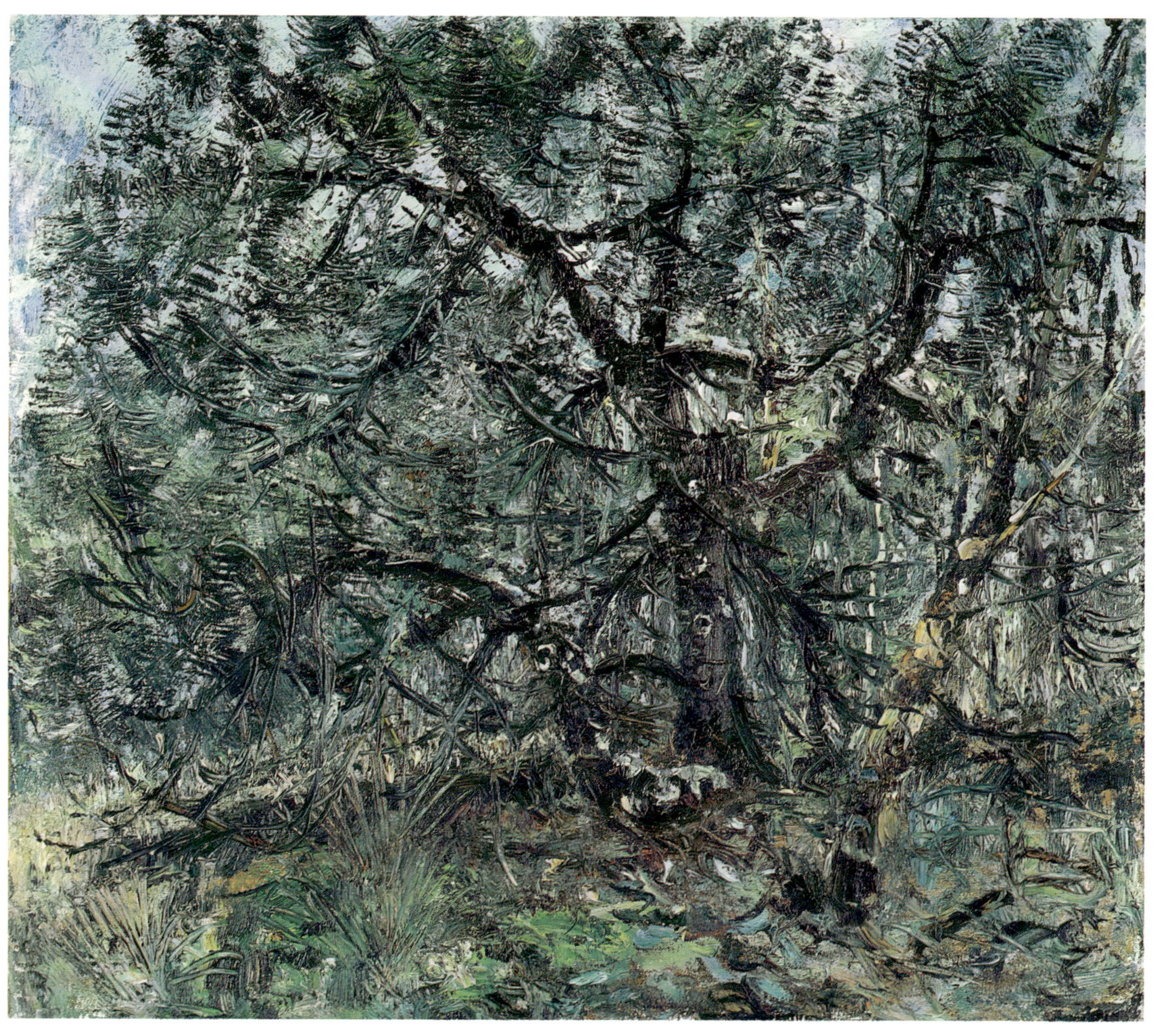

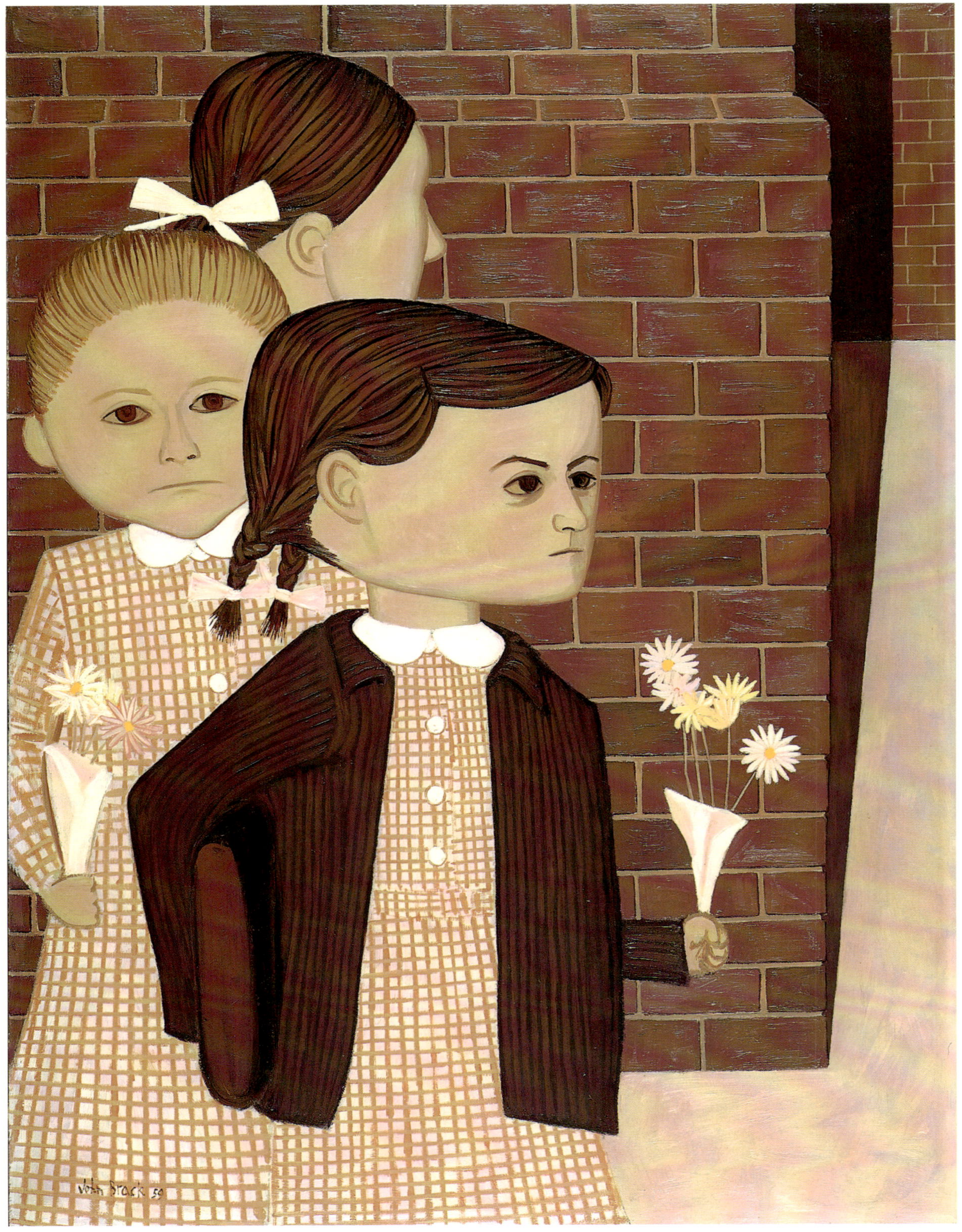

John Brack 50

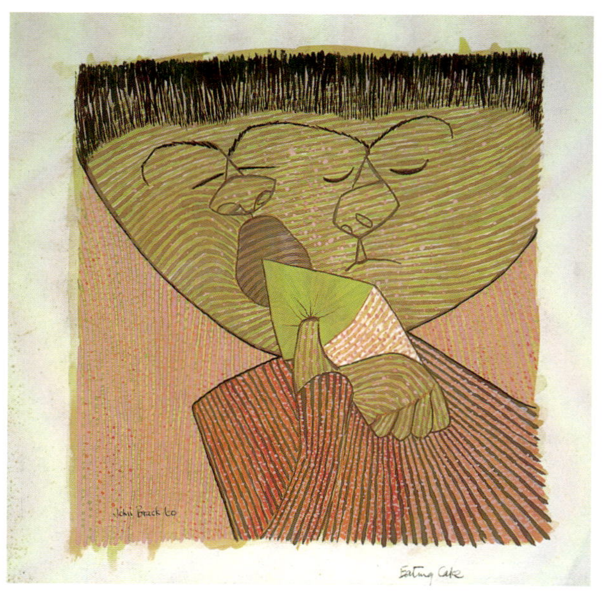

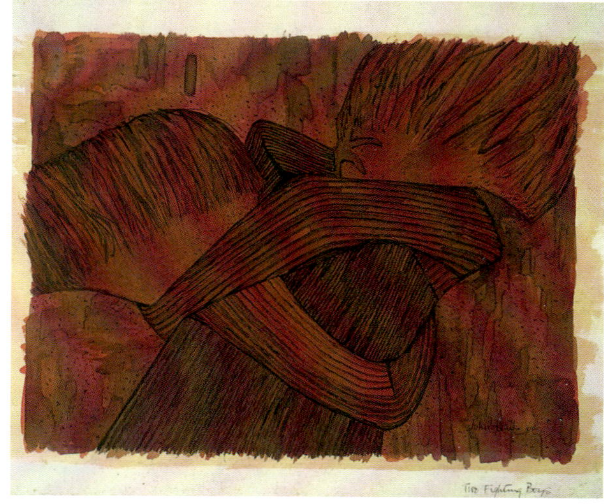

The diverse concerns of the Antipodeans are evident when comparing John Perceval's emotive landscapes with John Brack's incisive and intellectual paintings of the urban environment. Brack's *The girls at school* 1959 and *The playground* (small version) 1959 were shown in the Antipodeans exhibition. Both works are dispassionate representations of childhood. *The girls at school* captures the transitory moment at which the three girls enter the regimented environment of school. *The playground* (small version) defines the limits of this world. Here the viewer maintains a distanced objectivity and the individuality of the children is now lost. The playground establishes the physical boundaries, while girls and boys unconsciously determine their own segregation through the games they play almost as preparation for their different adult roles.[19]

No doubt John Brack's experiences of his own children at school, and his teaching position at Melbourne Grammar School which he held from 1952 to 1962, provided a foundation for these works. The more visually ambiguous nature of *Eating cake* and *Two fighting boys*, both of 1960, suggests a conscious reaction to his earlier involvement with the Antipodeans and a reassertion of his artistic independence.

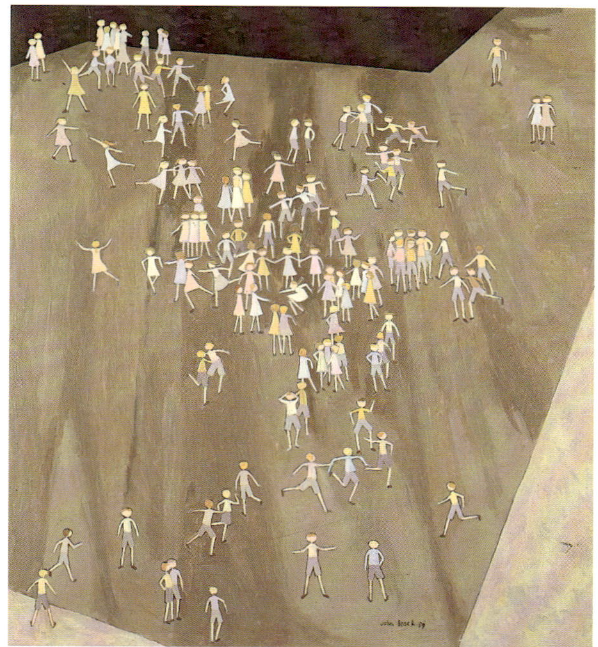

(opposite page) **John Brack** *The girls at school* 1959 oil on composition board 81.0 x 61.0 cm Collection, Elizabeth Summons
(this page above left) *Eating cake* 1960 watercolour and gouache on paper 47.8 x 47.0 cm
(above right) *Two fighting boys* 1960 watercolour and ink on paper 46.1 x 57.3 cm
(below) *The playground* (small version) 1959 oil on composition board   76.1 x 68.5 cm Kerry Stokes Collection, Perth

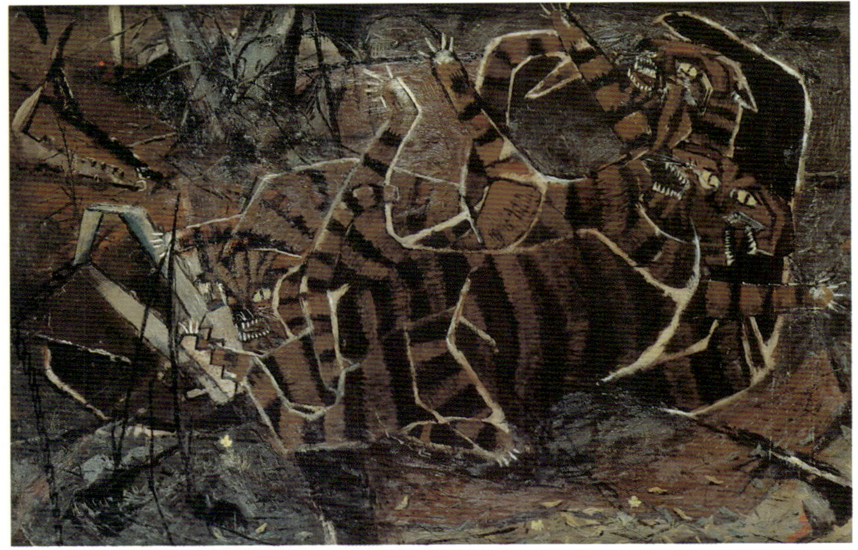

Clifton Pugh's work is fundamentally linked to his concern for the Australian bush. In the early 1950s he moved from the city to a tract of bushland at Cottles Bridge north east of Melbourne. Pugh's hostility towards thoughtless human behaviour and its consequences is highlighted in his works undertaken on the subject of the feral cat, such as *A cat in a rabbit-trap* 1957 — a response to the devastation wrought by these animals on native fauna. In this work the fragmented imagery reflects the violent struggle of the animal in an attempt to break free; the jawbone in the upper-left corner mirrors the clasping jaws of the trap and alludes to the inevitable conclusion. The rabbit-trap also refers indirectly to the damage caused by that other introduced animal — both the feral cat and the rabbit are symptomatic of the destructive cycle of human impact on the native bush.[20]

Pugh was the only artist to hang a portrait in the Antipodeans exhibition. *Portrait of an Australian artist* 1956 is a painting of the young Melbourne painter, Kevin Meynell. It is an early work that combines modernist pictorial concerns with a sensitive touch. Pugh's ability to capture the personality of his subjects in his portraits subsequently secured him the Archibald Prize in 1965, and again in 1971 and 1972.

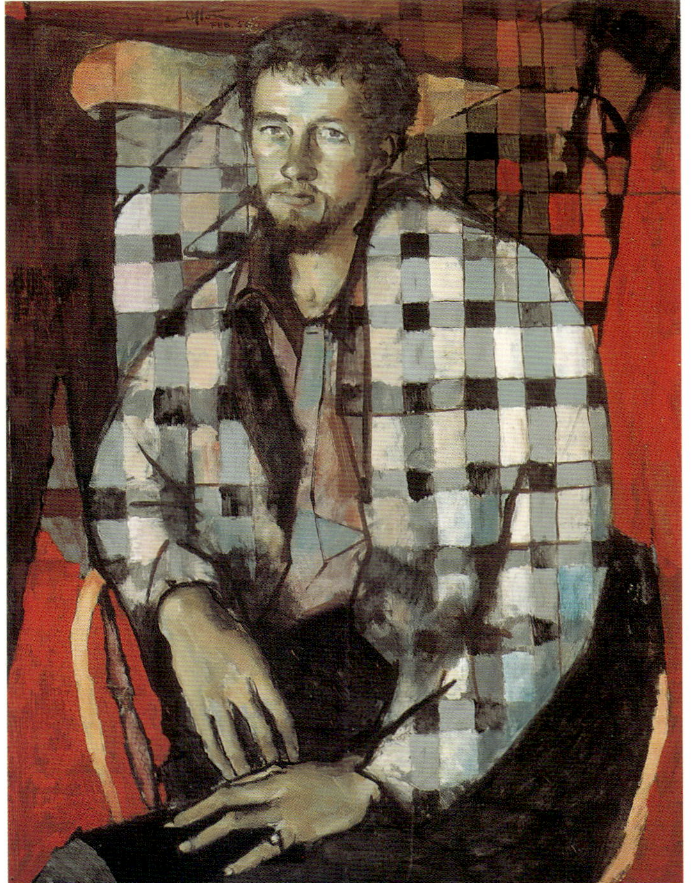

(above) **Clifton Pugh** *A cat in a rabbit-trap* 1957 oil on composition board 90.0 x 136.0 cm
(below) *Portrait of an Australian artist (Kevin Meynell)* 1956 oil on composition board 116.0 x 86.4 cm

While Robert Dickerson remained
on the fringe of the Sydney art scene
during the 1950s, he developed
strong associations with Melbourne
based artists and, in John Reed,
he found an early advocate. Reed
offered him his first solo exhibition
at the newly formed Gallery
of Contemporary Art in Melbourne
in 1956. It was these personal ties
that no doubt encouraged the
Antipodeans to invite Dickerson to
join them. His inclusion also partially
rectified the obvious Melbourne
weighting of the group. Dickerson
had recently held a major exhibition
in Sydney. The *Sydney Morning
Herald* claimed '[his] works of
powerful and sombre distinction are
the most exciting impact on
Australian painting by a young artist
since Nolan's first one-man show'.[21]

Dickerson's paintings of individuals
are not portraits; his nameless
subjects epitomise the experience
of social isolation in the urban
environment. *The bank clerk* 1959
was one of five works sent to
Melbourne for the Antipodeans
exhibition. The immediate impact
of its monumental simplicity forces
the psychological tension in the work
upon the viewer. The bank clerk is
half submerged in the gloom; a single
elongated shadow against the wall
heightens the sense of isolation.
His solemn mood also distances him
from the viewer. As an individual he
is a figure of resignation, alienated
both from the impersonal institution
he serves and the customers he deals
with lifelessly.

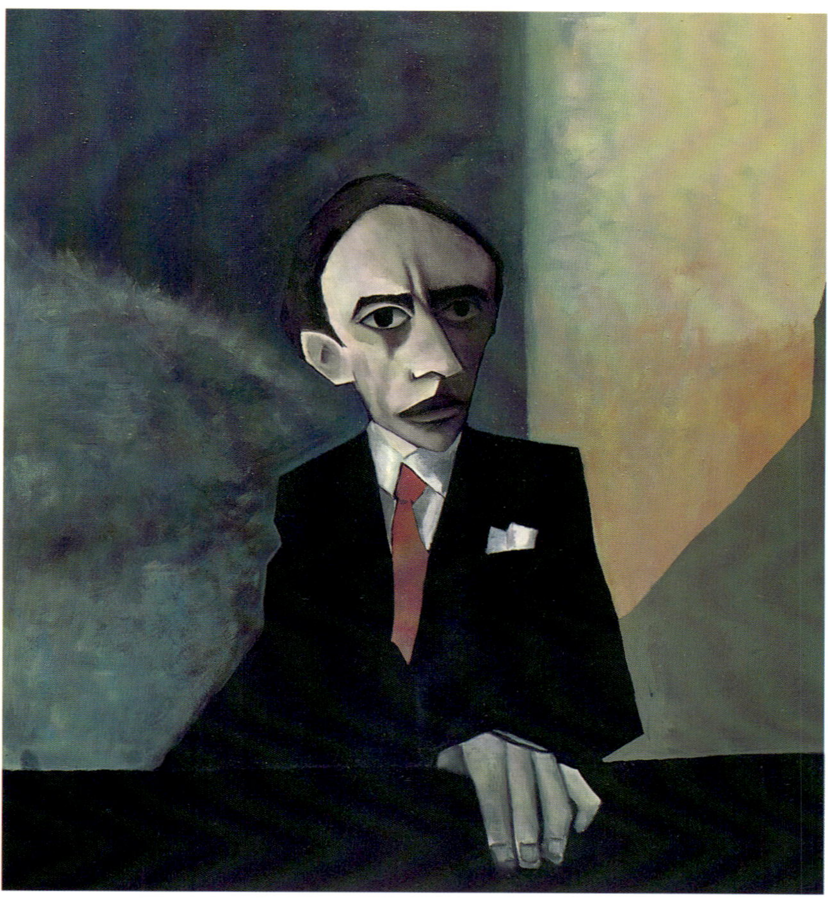

Robert Dickerson *The bank clerk* 1959 enamel on composition board 153.0 x 138.0 cm
The Holmes à Court Collection, Heytesbury

The Antipodeans created considerable controversy within artistic circles, yet their demise as a group was rapid. All were surprised by the degree of hostility directed towards them. Robert Dickerson and Clifton Pugh resigned shortly after the 1959 exhibition and Arthur Boyd set sail for London in November that year. As the possibility of a London show evaporated so did the commitment of the remaining members of the group. One last formal meeting was held in January 1960. John Brack resigned soon afterwards. Both Charles Blackman and David Boyd left for London in the early 1960s after winning prestigious prizes (Blackman, the Helena Rubenstein Travelling Scholarship in 1960, and Boyd, the Italian Government Art Scholarship for 1961). Each of the former Antipodeans continued to pursue his own path, yet their one exhibition together, and the one document, had bound them as a group into the story of Australian art.

Steve Tonkin

1   Bernard Smith, 'A New Art Group – The Antipodeans', *CAS Broadsheet*, no.2, May 1959, p.5.

2   For discussion of the Antipodeans and 'The Antipodean Manifesto' within the history of Australian painting see Bernard Smith, *Australian Painting 1788–1990*, Melbourne: Oxford University Press, 1992, pp.289–332; Robert Hughes, *The Art of Australia* (rev. edn), Melbourne: Penguin, 1970, pp.221–250. In most monographs on the artists involved in the Antipodeans, discussion is made about their involvement in the group; two of the most important articles on the Antipodeans are, Barbara Blackman, 'The Antipodean Affair', *Art and Australia*, vol.5, no.4, March 1968, pp.607–616; Deborah Haycraft, 'The Making of a Manifesto', *Art and Australia*, vol.26, no.2, Summer 1988, pp.284—289. The most recent exhibition to revisit the Antipodeans was held in 1988–89, *The Antipodeans: Another Chapter*, Lauraine Diggins Fine Arts, Melbourne, 1988. Bernard Smith has written extensively on the Antipodeans, see, most importantly, Bernard Smith, 'The Truth about the Antipodeans' (1984), reprinted in his *The Death of the Artist as Hero*, Melbourne: Oxford University Press, 1988, pp.198–213; see also G. Catalano, *The Years of Hope: Australian art and criticism, 1959–1968*, Melbourne: Oxford University Press, 1981. For a comprehensive analysis of the Melbourne art scene between 1946–1968, including a discussion on the Antipodeans, see Christopher Heathcote, *A Quiet Revolution: The rise of Australian art 1946–1968*, Melbourne: The Text Publishing Co., 1995.

3   Bernard Smith recalls that Leonard French, Noel Counihan and Fred Williams were suggested as potential members at this first meeting. Other possible members were discussed by the remaining Antipodeans at the last meeting on 29 January 1960. Jon Molvig, Albert Tucker, Sidney Nolan and Fred Williams were considered; see Bernard Smith, 'The Truth about the Antipodeans' (1984), in his *The Death of the Artist as Hero*, p.201.

4   Bernard Smith, 'The Antipodean Intervention', in his *The Critic as Advocate*, Melbourne: Oxford University Press, 1989, p.137. The name 'Antipodean Brotherhood' was considered briefly.

5   'Artbursts — Antipodeans', *Bulletin*, 19 August 1959, pp.24–25.

6   For a discussion of Bernard Smith's attempt to secure a London venue for the Antipodeans, see Bernard Smith, 'The Truth about the Antipodeans', in his *The Death of the Artist as Hero*, pp.209–212.

7   ibid, p.204.

8   From 'The Antipodean Manifesto', in *Antipodeans 4th–15th Aug. 1959*, Victorian Artists' Society, Melbourne, 1959.

9   Barbara Blackman, 'The Antipodean Affair', p.615.

10 Bernard Smith, 'The Truth about the Antipodeans', in his *The Death of the Artist as Hero*, pp.198–213.

11 Arnold Shore, 'Charles Blackman Stands Alone', *Age*, 4 August 1959, p.2; 'Artbursts—Antipodeans', *Bulletin*, 19 August 1959, pp.24–25; 'The Antipodeans', *Modern Art News*, vol.1, no.1, 1959, pp.9–10; Franz Philipp, 'Antipodeans Aweigh', *Nation*, no.25, 29 August 1959, pp.18–19; Alan McCulloch, 'Battle cry of Antipodeans', *Herald*, 5 August 1959, p.23. Alan McCulloch, 'Figurative — or Abstract?', *Herald*, 12 August 1959, p.25.

12 Bernard Smith, *Australian Painting 1788–1960*, Chapter 9: 'Figurative and Non-figurative 1950–60', pp.289–332.

13 *Nine Sydney Artists*, Gallery A, Melbourne, 1961; the artists involved were John Olsen, William Rose, Stanislaus Rapotec, Leonard Hessing, Clement Meadmore, Eric Smith, Peter Upward, Hector Gilliland and Carl Plate

14 The National Gallery of Australia has recently acquired Arthur Boyd's *Reflected bride 1* 1958, see Tim Fisher, 'New Acquisition: Arthur Boyd, *Reflected bride 1* 1958', *artonview*, no.19, Spring 1999, pp.26–27.

15 Franz Philipp, *Arthur Boyd*, London: Thames and Hudson, p.83.

16 David Boyd 'Statement', Smith Papers, cited in Deborah Haycraft, 'The Making of a Manifesto', p.286; this statement was not included in the final version of the Manifesto.

17 Alan McCulloch, 'Angels in ceramics', *Herald*, 3 September 1958, p.24.

18 For further discussion, see Margaret Plant, *John Perceval*, (rev.edn), Melbourne: Lansdowne, 1978, p.78

19 For an extended discussion of these works and others exhibited by Brack at the Antipodeans exhibition, see Sasha Grishin, *The Art of John Brack*, Melbourne: Oxford University Press, 1990, pp.70–73.

20 For further discussion, see Traudi Allen, *Clifton Pugh, Patterns of a lifetime*, Melbourne: Thomas Nelson, 1981, pp.58–63.

21 'Remarkable Paintings by Robert Dickerson', *Sydney Morning Herald*, 13 May 1959, p.2.

TACHISTES, ACTION PAINTERS, GEOMETRIC ABSTRACTIONISTS, ABSTRACT EXPRESSIONISTS AND THEIR INNUMERABLE BAND OF CAMP FOLLOWERS

Today *tachistes,* action painters, geometric abstractionists, abstract expressionists and their innumerable band of camp followers threaten to benumb the intellect and wit of art with their bland and pretentious mysteries. The art which they champion is not an art sufficient for our time, it is not an art for living men. It reveals, it seems to us, a death of the mind and spirit.

('The Antipodean Manifesto', Melbourne, August 1959[1])

The 'Antipodean affair'[2] has resonated so loudly down the years since the *Antipodeans* exhibition of 1959 and its accompanying Manifesto that the oppositions it invoked are embedded in our understanding of the art of the 1950s and 60s: figuration/ abstraction; Melbourne/ Sydney; local/ international; conservative/ progressive.

The Antipodean challenge was a gesture towards securing a place in history: the exhibition and Bernard Smith's Manifesto presented figuration in art as central to an authentic contemporary Australian ethos. This claim did not go unchallenged. The important exhibition of the '9 Sydney artists' of 1961, held in Sydney and in Melbourne, was a riposte, and there were others. In the early 1960s abstract and semi-abstract Australian art was asserting its place in local cultural traditions and looking further afield. Non-figurative artists were winning prizes and travelling scholarships in increasing numbers. In London in 1961 at the Whitechapel Art Gallery, the exhibition *Recent Australian Painting* — a major show with over a hundred works by fifty-five artists — represented abstract art and figurative art in about equal numbers. The organisation of this exhibition scuttled the ambitions of Bernard Smith and the Antipodean artists for their own London showing as the singular voice of Australian art.

The context for the apparent rearguard action of the Antipodean group was their concern at the inroads being made by non-figurative, non-objective and abstract art in Australia, particularly in Sydney — Melbourne's strong tradition of figurative art has long been a defining feature of the differences between the two cities' art practices. In 'The Antipodean Manifesto' it was implicit that Melbourne was unaffected by abstract art: 'wherever we look, New York, Paris, London, San Francisco or *Sydney*, we see young artists dazzled by the luxurious pageantry and colour of non-figuration'.[3] Throughout the 1950s there had been influential shows in Sydney of abstract and semi-abstract art, such as Ralph Balson and Robert Klippel's joint exhibition at Macquarie Galleries in 1952, and *Direction* 1 at Macquarie Galleries in 1956, which included Klippel, John Olsen, John Passmore, William Rose and Eric Smith.

By the end of the decade there was a real diversity of non-figurative art practices in Sydney and, to a lesser degree, in Melbourne. The position on non-figurative art taken in 'The Antipodean Manifesto' overlooked this diversity, and the speculative abstract investigations of artists as various as Fred Williams, Leonard French, John Olsen, John Passmore and Peter Upward were grouped as a single camp — the other.

The aim of *The Antipodeans: Challenge and response in Australian art 1955–1965* is to place the art of the Antipodean group within its proper context, alongside the broad sweep of non-figurative Australian art, leading up to and beyond the Antipodean challenge.[4] All seven Antipodean artists are represented,[5] and twenty-six others.

In her catalogue essay for *New Directions 1952–
1962*, Christine France makes the point that 'the idea
of a new art movement simply arriving in a country is
simplistic',[6] and that the history of abstraction in
Australia developed as a result of interaction between
local conditions and influences from abroad.

Twentieth-century Australian experiments with
abstraction go back to 1919, when Roland Wakelin
and Roy de Maistre briefly took up a form of painting
called synchromism — a derivation of post-
impressionism based on the generation of form through
pure colour. Wakelin and de Maistre's investigations
into the relationships between music theory and colour
theory linked their work with the aesthetic of early
abstract painters, in particular Wassily Kandinsky.
In Melbourne in the 1930s, Sam Atyeo made paintings
influenced by the linear abstractions of Paul Klee,
before leaving Australia forever in 1935.

The establishment of the Crowley–Fizelle art school
in Sydney in 1932 began a vital period of abstract
investigation amongst a group of committed and
talented artists including Grace Crowley, Rah Fizelle,
Ralph Balson, Frank and Margel Hinder, Dorrit Black,
and Gerald and Margo Lewers. These artists shared
a general assumption 'that pure abstraction imaged
the underlying order of creation'.[7] Most of the group
had direct experience of modern movements overseas:
Crowley had studied cubism in France with Albert
Gleizes and André Lhôte; and the Hinders became
closely involved with the work and theories of cubism,
futurism, the Bauhaus and the Mexican muralists
during their seven years in America. In 1939 the group
staged *Exhibition 1* at David Jones Gallery, Sydney.
The catalogue foreword was written by Eleonore Lange,
a sculptor and teacher from Germany whose influential
lectures and writings 'did much to raise the level of
understanding in art in Sydney … and played a most
significant role in creating an informed audience for
contemporary art'.[8] She wrote: 'Painting today is
abandoning the representation of objects in order
to establish a new realm of visual experience.'[9]

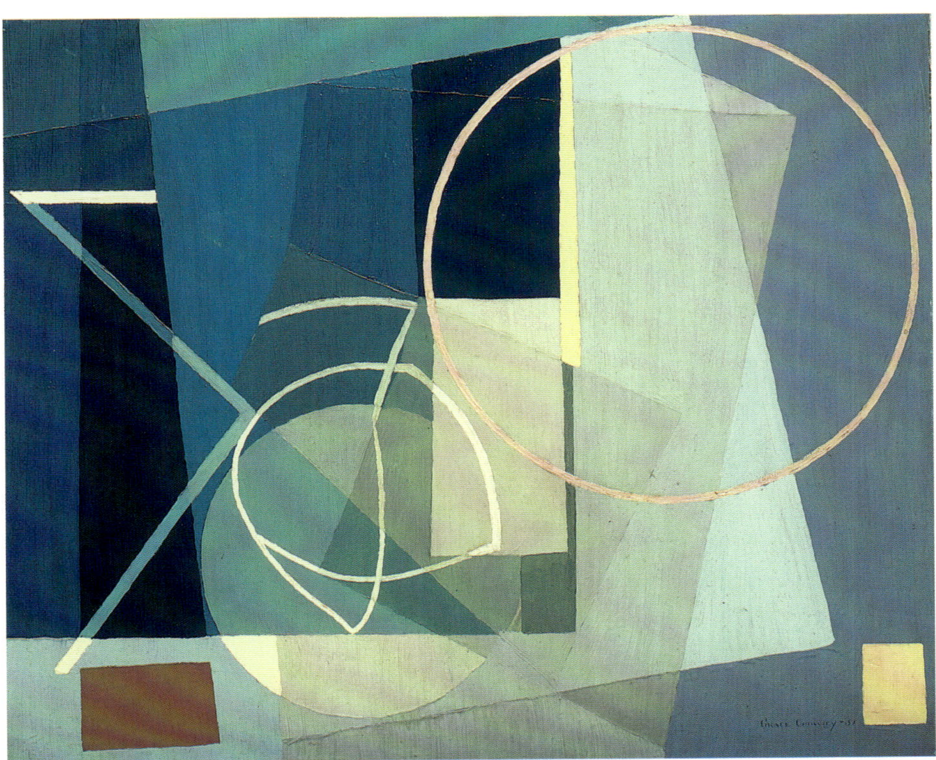

Grace Crowley *Painting* 1951 oil on composition board 58.4 x 70.6 cm

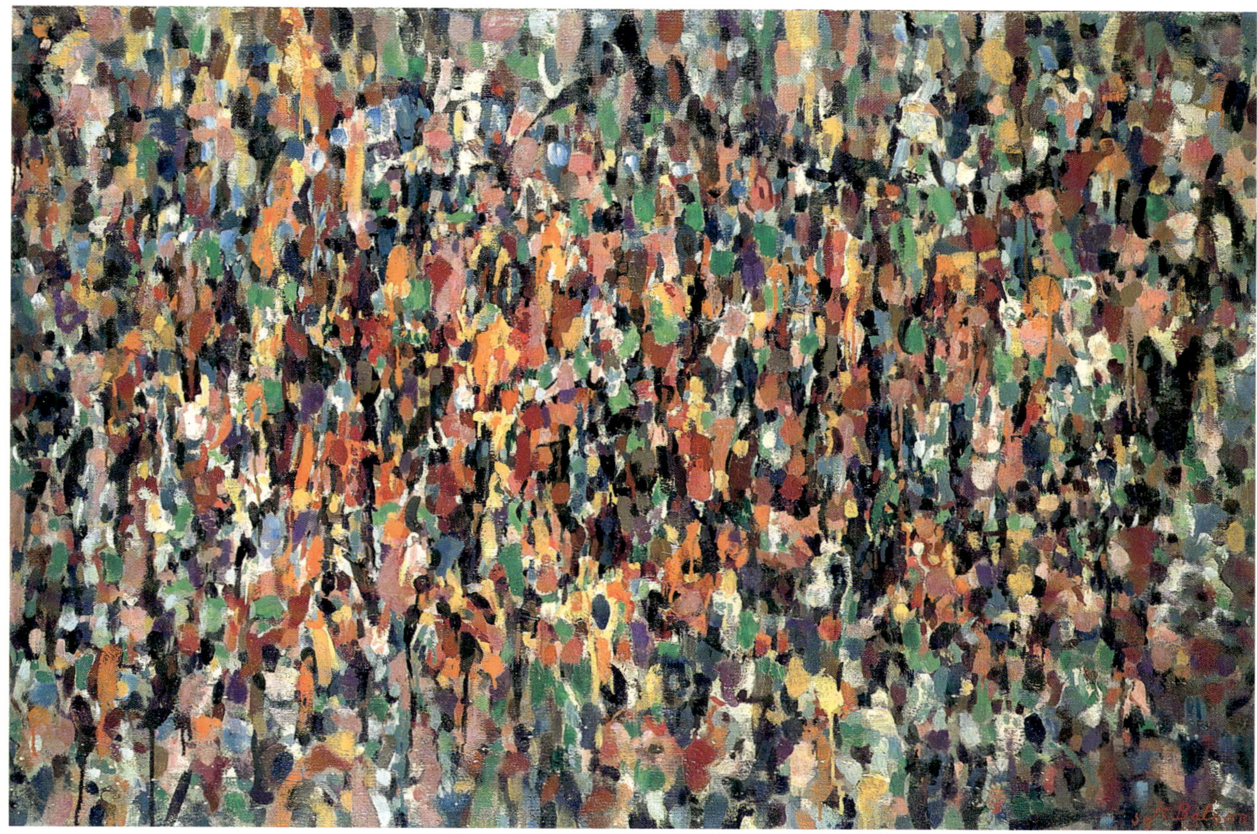

Ralph Balson *Non-objective painting* 1959 enamel on composition board 91.5 x 137.5 cm

The Second World War effectively broke up this group, but Grace Crowley and Ralph Balson continued to move towards purely abstract painting through the 1940s and 1950s. In the early 1950s both were making confident and sophisticated paintings exploring form. These works, such as Crowley's *Painting*1951 and *Abstract painting* 1952, are characterised by dynamic colour and finely balanced tonal relationships.

In the late 1950s Balson's adherence to cubist structure and the harmonies of Mondrian was succeeded by a far more painterly approach in his work, as he became increasingly interested in a theory of the universe derived from Albert Einstein. In Balson's *Non-objective*

Paintings of the late 1950s the surfaces are shimmering fields of unified colour, representing for the artist 'a universe without beginning, without end; a continuous, creating, destroying and expanding movement'.[10] His last major series of works, the *Matter Paintings*, shows the influence of his first overseas trip to Europe and New York, undertaken in 1960 when he was seventy. Contact with textural painting, in particular Tachism and the work of Burri and Tapiès, led Balson to experiments in pouring and swirling on the surfaces of his paintings, creating fluid rhythmic effects. In these late works the artist's vision of the order of the universe devolved from structured harmony, through relativity to organised chaos.

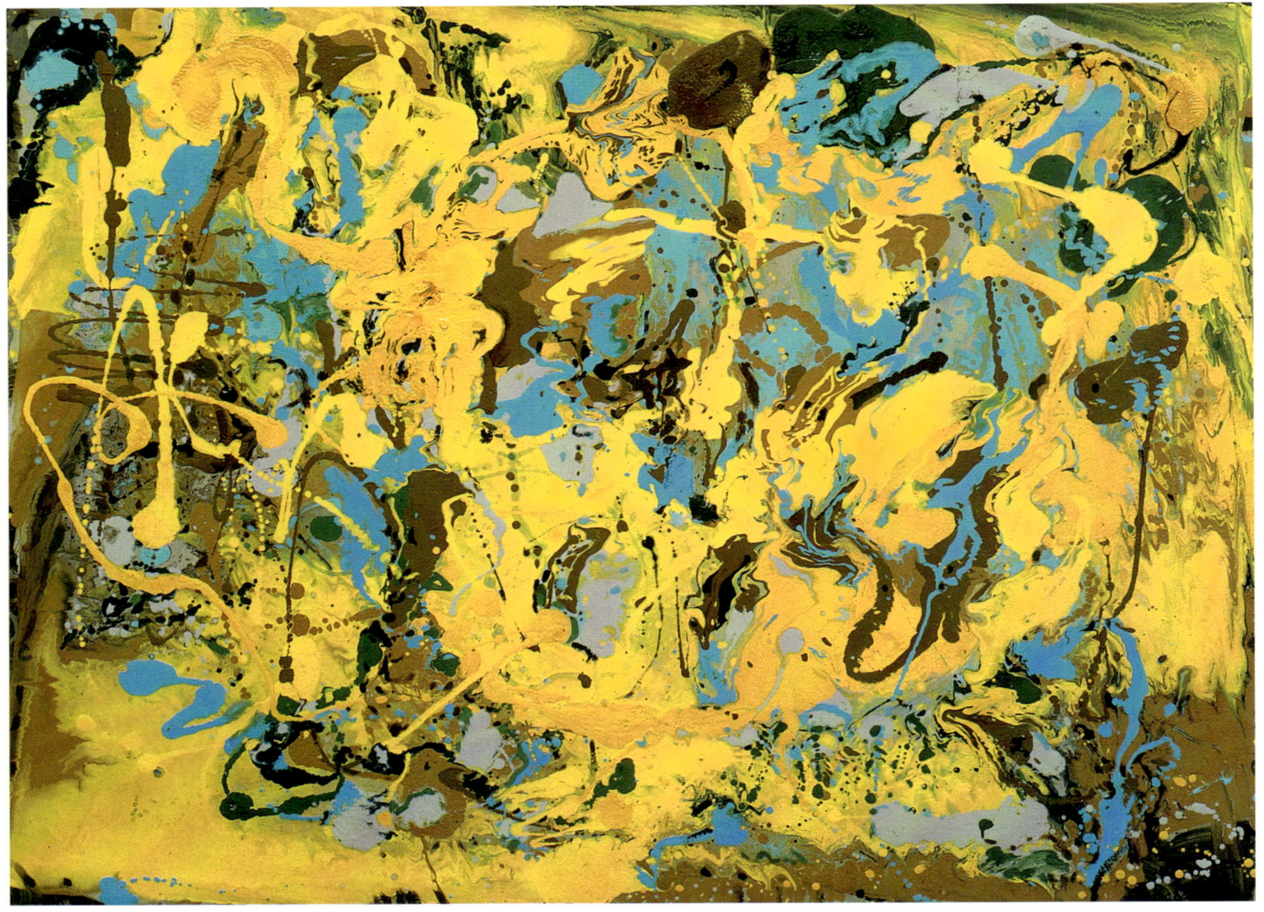

Ralph Balson *Matter painting* 1960 enamel on composition board 91.3 x 122.2 cm

Balson, in his sixties during the 1950s, was one of a number of senior Australian artists who, through their practice, exerted influence on younger artists. A quiet figure and not a teacher, Balson exhibited throughout the 1950s and 60s, individually and in group shows, and was included in a number of significant survey exhibitions of contemporary Australian art.[11] His joint exhibition with Robert Klippel at Macquarie Galleries in 1952 demonstrates his relevance for the generation of the 1950s — Klippel was his junior by thirty years.

In the 1950s and 60s Godfrey Miller, Ian Fairweather and John Passmore were revered as practitioners and influential teachers to a younger generation. Like Balson, Miller and Fairweather were born in the early 1890s, Passmore a decade later in 1904. All had travelled extensively and brought a rich variety of artistic and cultural influences to the Australian scene.

Godfrey Miller's work shifted between abstraction and representation, but the ostensible subjects of his paintings — still lifes, landscapes, and figures — were merely devices for his endless examination of the nature of form. His art appears to dissolve before our eyes, but in the worked and reworked surfaces of his paintings structure emerges. In *Blue unity* 1954–55, one of his more abstract paintings, the strong vertical and horizontal lines formed by intricate and labour-intensive grids reflect Miller's early architectural training in New Zealand. The painting is a construction made of myriad squares and rectangles of subtle colour.

Miller's debt to cubism is evident in his work; he had also absorbed influences from travels in the Middle East, China and Japan which contributed to a philosophy based on equilibrium and the balance of tensions. Miller taught at East Sydney Technical College for many years, and although his output was small and he managed to sustain a kind of reclusiveness within the city, his work was widely admired by students and contemporaries. In 1959 — the year of the Antipodeans exhibition — a retrospective exhibition of Miller's work was held at the National Gallery of Victoria.

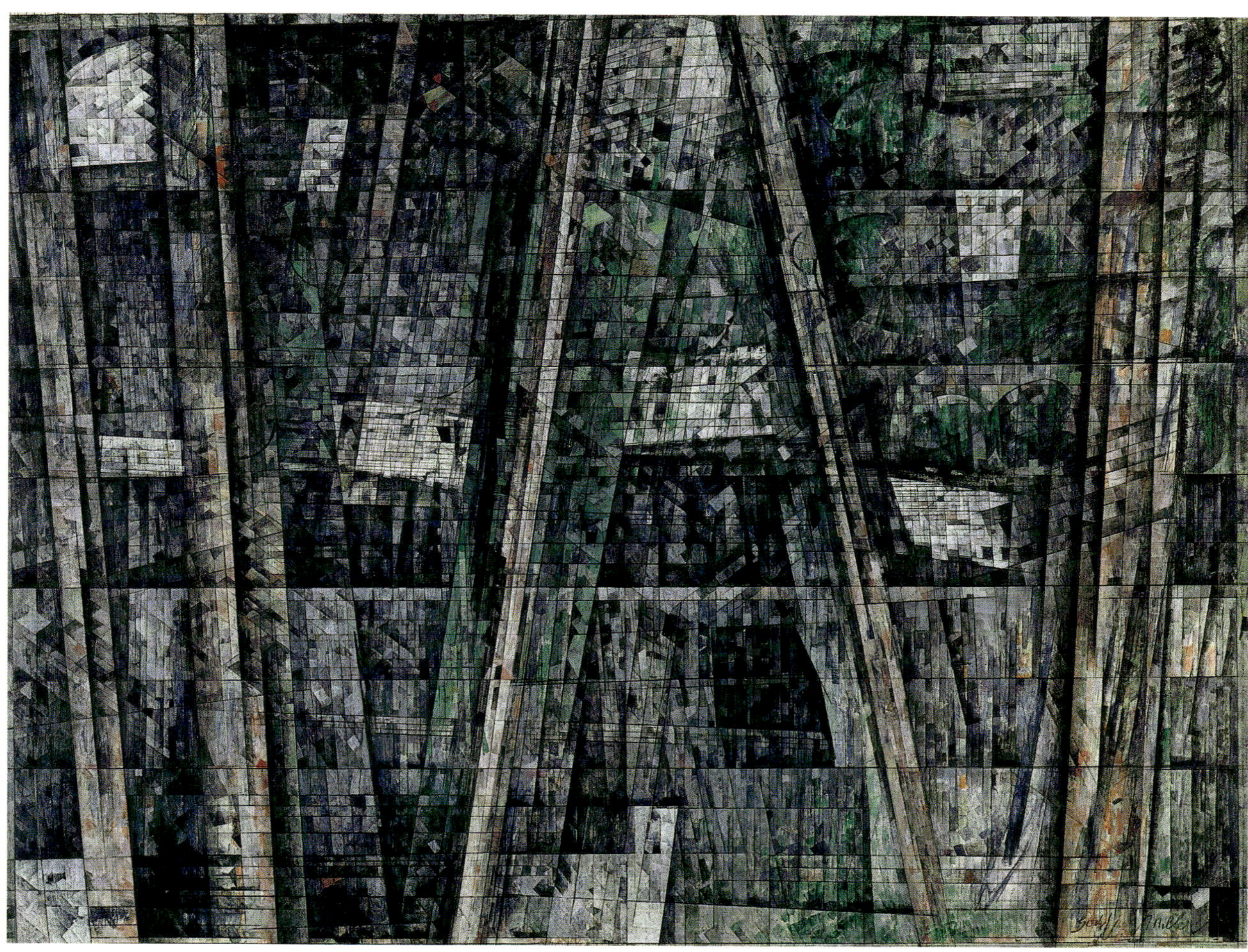

Godfrey Miller *Blue unity* 1954–55 oil on canvas 69.8 x 88.2 cm

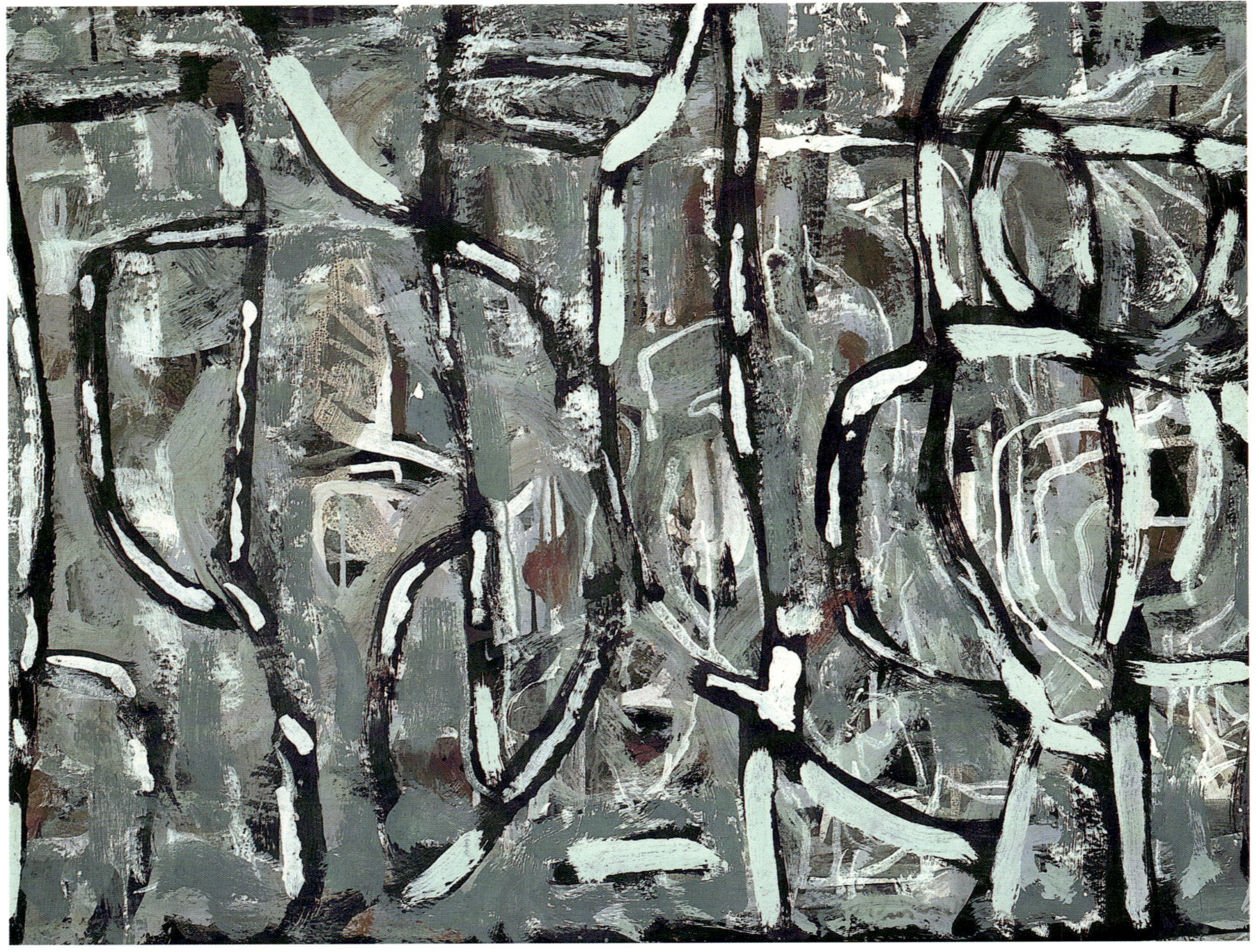

Ian Fairweather *Composition* 1961 gouache and synthetic polymer paint on cardboard mounted on composition board 69.5 x 70.1 cm
Gift of Lucy Swanton 1981 © Ian Fairweather, 1961/DACS. Reproduced by permission of VISCOPY Ltd, Sydney 1999

Godfrey Miller and Ian Fairweather were described by James Gleeson in 1963 as occupying 'positions of lonely eminence'.[12] If this were true of Miller in Sydney, then it was doubly true of Fairweather, working in solitude on Bribie Island in Queensland. To young artists he was 'the painter's painter': his austere lifestyle and unique vision encapsulated the ideal romantic vision of an authentic creative spirit.

Fairweather brought together the influence of his training at the Slade School in London and pictorial conventions imbibed during his remarkable and extensive travels in the 1930s and 40s through China, Japan, Indonesia, India, Malaysia and the Pacific. This journeying, which ended when he settled on Bribie Island, provided the source material for Fairweather's work — the dense crowded patterning of landscapes, figures and temples which seem to elude representation or, at most, suggest it. His style is based on a calligraphic line which skates across the surface of his paintings, pushing the many layers of colour in and out in a roving, restless, complex web. In a 1963 interview with Hazel de Berg, Fairweather remarked: 'Painting to me is something of a tightrope act; it is between representation and the other thing — whatever that is. It is difficult to keep one's balance.'[13]

John Passmore returned to Sydney in
1950 after seventeen years in Europe.
He became one of Sydney's most
influential art teachers, first at the
Julian Ashton Art School and, from
1956, at East Sydney Technical
College. His students included
John Olsen, William Rose and
Yvonne Audette. In his painting
Passmore pursued an obsessive search
for structure and totality based on a
lifelong passion for the work of
Cézanne — his subject, the marine life
around Sydney Harbour, its bays,
its bathers and its fishing.

Composition c.1957–58 was painted
after Passmore exhibited in the group
show *Direction 1* at the Macquarie
Galleries in 1956. During this time
he became influenced by the work
of his students, in particular Olsen
and Audette, and his painting in the
late 1950s became more abstract
in form.[14] *Composition* has points of
reference to structure and represented
space, but without identifiable imagery.

Passmore's fling with pure abstraction
did not last, but in his teaching he was
a catalyst for the development of
abstraction, encouraging his students
to push the boundaries of their work
in ways he was hesitant to attempt.

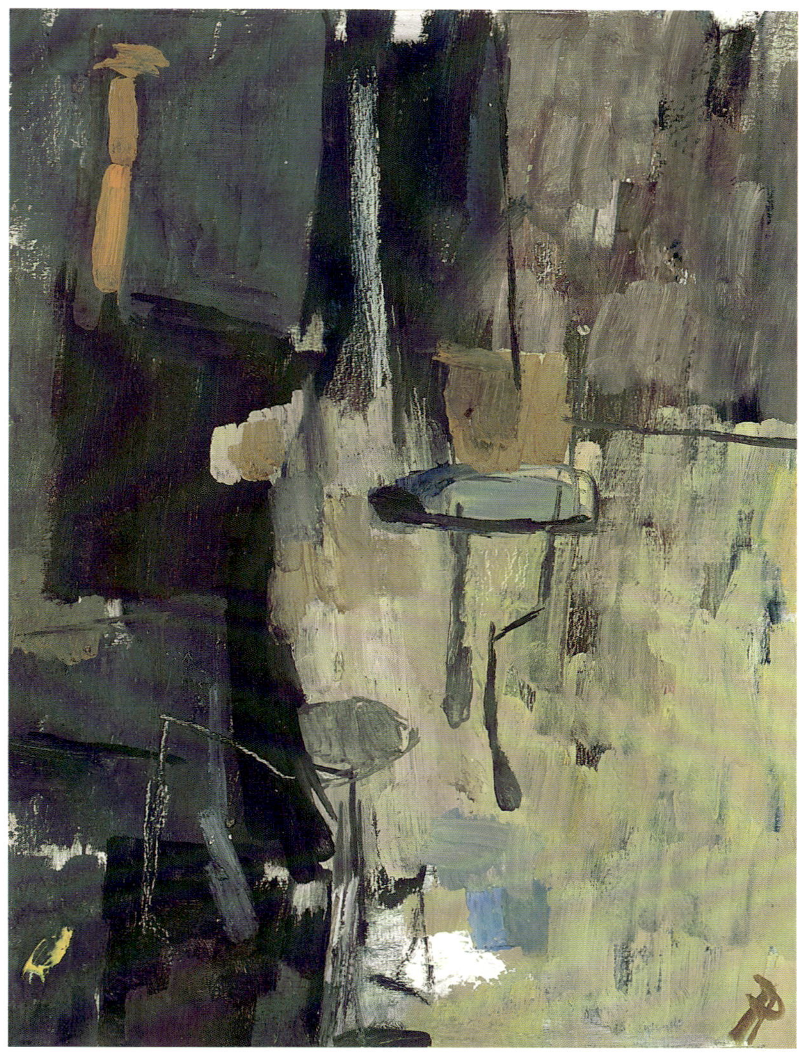

John Passmore *Composition* c.1957–58 oil on cardboard 50.0 x 37.6 cm
Reproduced courtesy of Elinor Wrobel, trustee

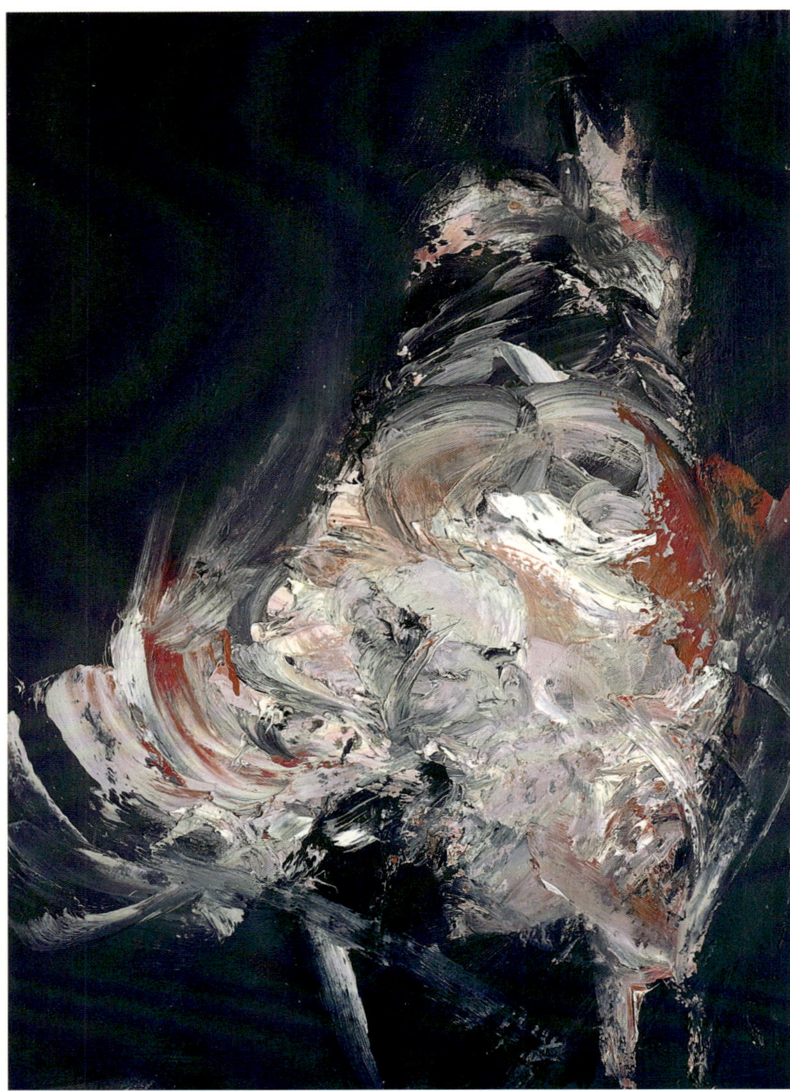

Stacha Halpern *Boeuf* 1961 oil on cardboard 76.0 x 53.0 cm

Greater exposure to contemporary international art in the 1950s came through significant travelling exhibitions, the arrival of émigré artists from Europe after the war, and the opportunities provided by newly established travelling scholarships. The most important exhibition of overseas art to come to Australia after the war was *French Painting Today*, which toured the capital cities during 1953. The show included work by major figures such as Picasso, Braque, Matisse, Chagall, Derain, Dufy and Ernst, as well as younger painters of the post-war period — André Marchand, Pierre Soulages, Hans Hartung, Nicholas de Staël and Vieira da Silva. For many Australian artists it was the work of this latter group that resonated; as John Olsen later said: 'What they seemed to represent was a natural progression from Cézanne like touches to a world less possessed by objectivity, more ethereal, more spiritual.'[15]

The impact of *French Painting Today* reinforced in Australia an idea of Europe as the natural source for vanguardism, particularly in the post-war period. Since 1939 immigrant European artists such as Stacha Halpern, Stanislaus Rapotec, Henry Salkauskas and Leonard Hessing had contributed significantly to local knowledge of contemporary art movements.[16] Halpern came to Australia from Poland in 1939, aged twenty, and his vigorous and arresting forms in paintings and pottery had an impact on art in Melbourne during the 1940s. He spent the years from 1951 to 1966 in Europe, and had considerable success as an artist, exhibiting widely and becoming well known in Paris, where *Boeuf* 1961 was painted.

In the increasingly affluent 1950s more Australian artists were able to travel overseas, either under their own steam or with the benefit of government and private patronage. Janet Dawson was awarded the National Gallery of Victoria Travelling Scholarship in 1956 and spent several years in Europe, studying in England, travelling in Italy, and working as a lithographer in Paris. The *Italian Landscape* drawings she made in Anticoli Corrado near Rome in 1960 are abstracted lyrical responses to the landscape, influenced by European surrealism and the warmth of abstract painting by artists such as Mark Rothko whose work Dawson had seen at the Tate Gallery in 1959.

Dawson returned to Australia in 1960 with an informed understanding of new movements in abstraction in Europe. She became closely involved with Gallery A in Melbourne, as an exhibitor and curator, and in 1963 she established the Gallery A print workshop. Founded by Max Hutchinson and Clement Meadmore in 1959, Gallery A was an outlet for contemporary design which rapidly became a lively focus for abstract art.

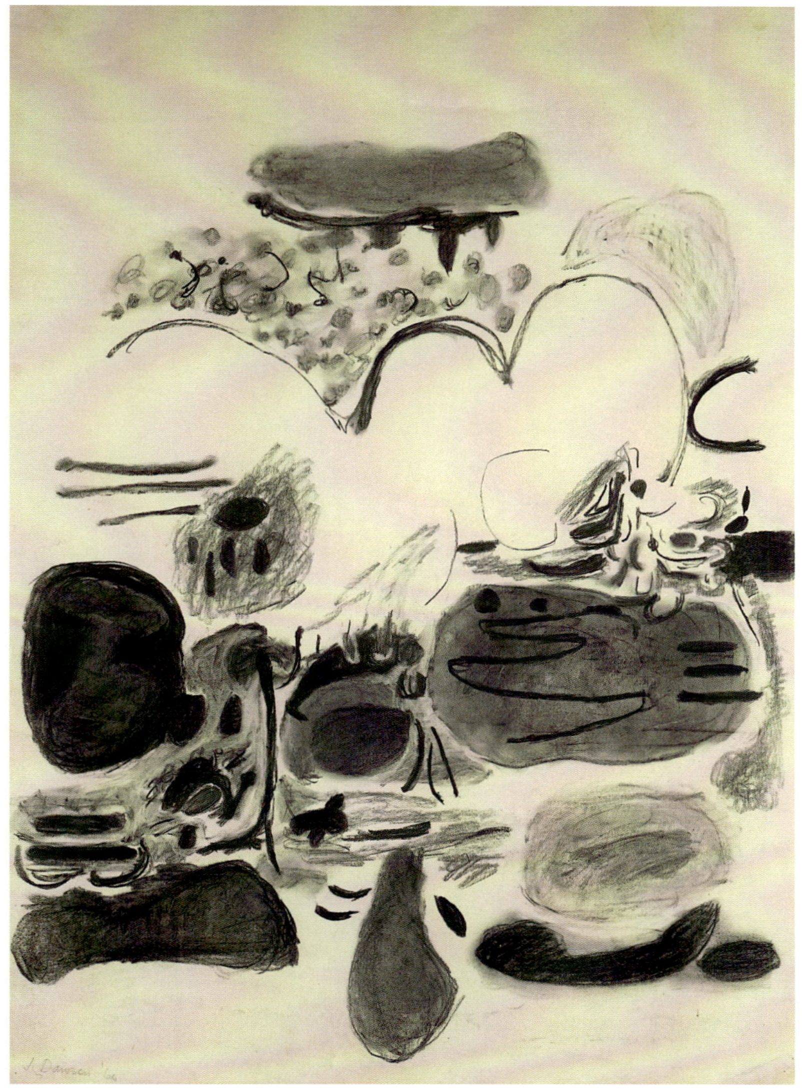

Janet Dawson *Italian landscape drawing* 1960 charcoal on paper 100.0 x 70.0 cm
© Janet Dawson, 1960. Reproduced by permission of VISCOPY Ltd, Sydney 1999.

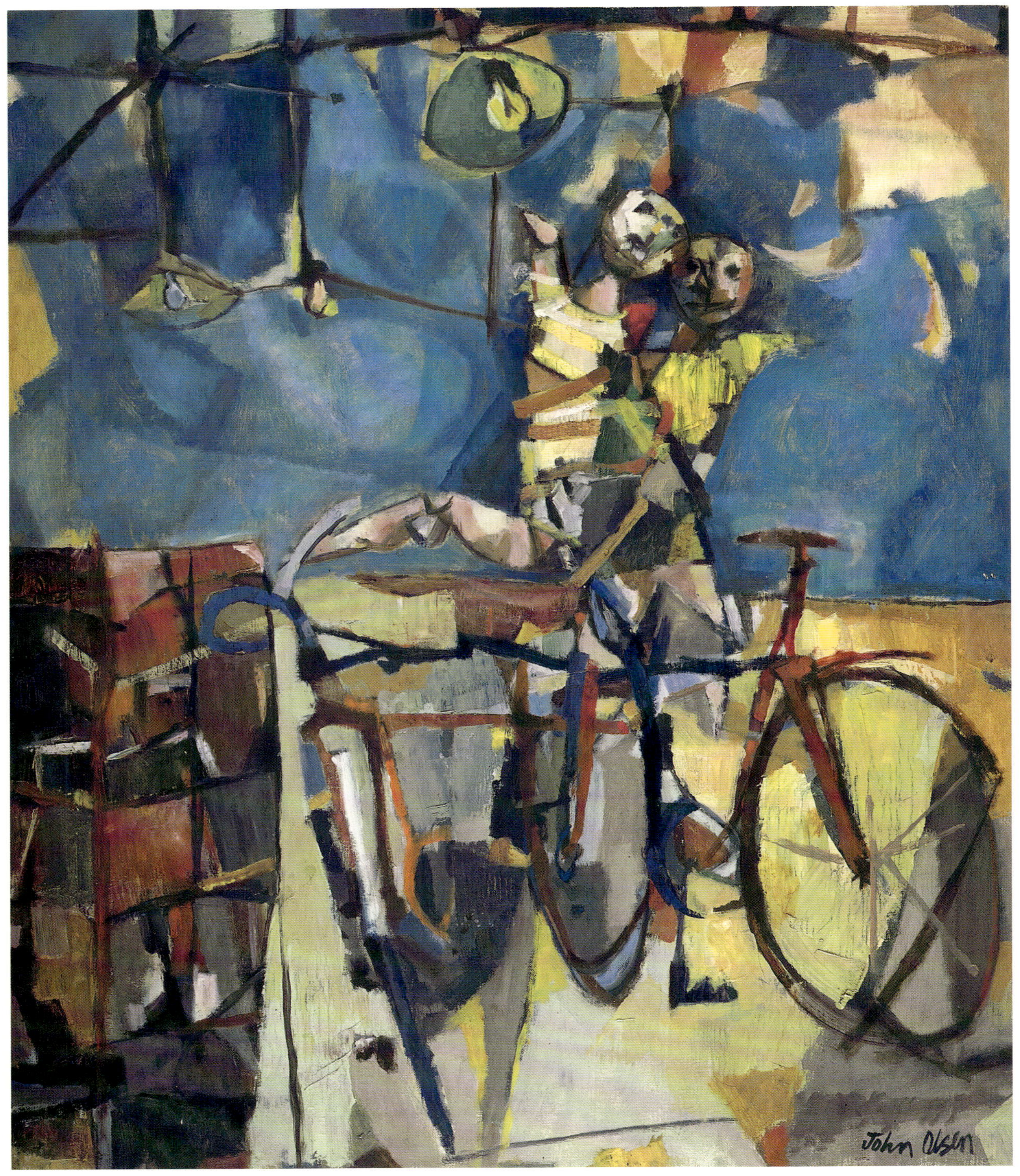

John Olsen was the recipient of a private scholarship
in 1956 which enabled him to spend three years based
in Spain. His first important exhibition was in 1955,
the year the *Bicycle Boys* series was painted,
and although his paintings showed the influence of
his teacher, John Passmore, Olsen's lyrical, linear style
had an effervescence which had more in common
with Paul Klee than Passmore's examplar, Cézanne.

The figures rapidly disappeared from Olsen's work
in the mid 1950s: between *Bicycle boys* 1955 and
Bush walk 1957 the work seems to leap out of its skin,
as Olsen's exuberant line abstracted. His subject
became the landscape of Australia, particularly Sydney,
and the paintings describe the experience of landscape
rather than its visual appearance.

Olsen's European sojourn brought various influences
to his work, which he was able to translate into an
Australian idiom; his bouncing line became consciously
childlike, possibly through his association with Dubuffet
and the COBRA group in Paris.[17] *January 14 1960*
1960 belongs to a group of works influenced by
textural painting and incorporates beeswax and
various pigments in its scarred and skeined surface.
Its monumental form and sombre simplicity were not
to be repeated in Olsen's work, and *Bush walk*,
which was exhibited in the Whitechapel exhibition
of 1961, is more characteristic of his marriage
of modernism with the Australian landscape.
James Gleeson noted in 1963 that 'the characteristics
of this country are as implicit in the abstracts of John
Olsen as they are explicit in the landscapes of Nolan'.[18]

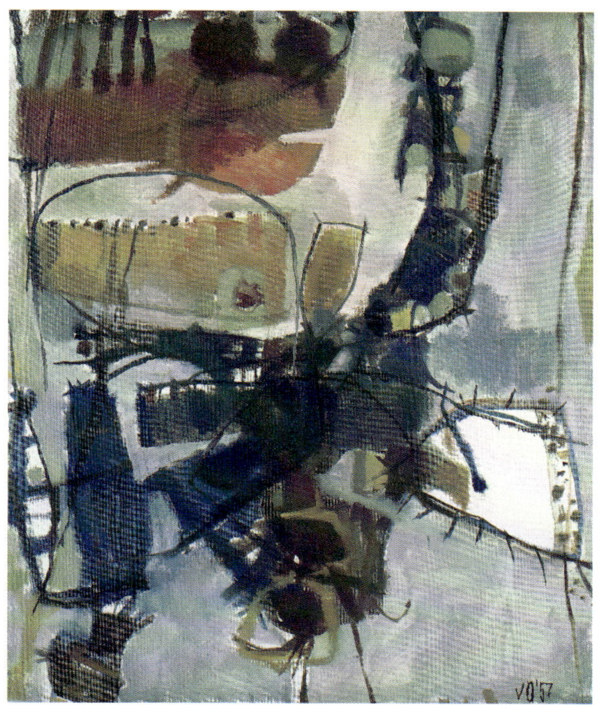

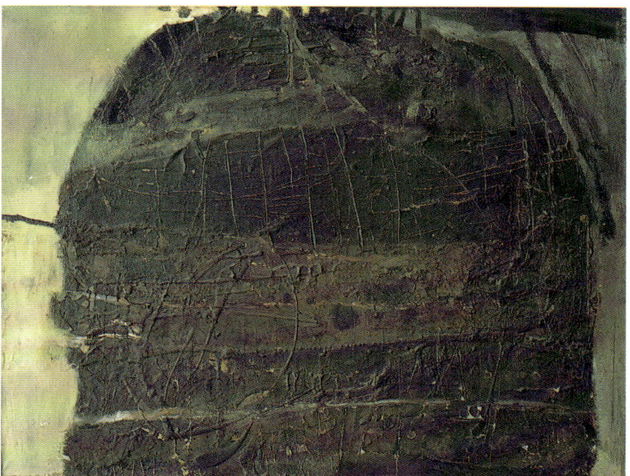

(opposite page) **John Olsen** *Bicycle boys* 1955 oil on canvas
92.5 x 77.2 cm
(this page above) *Bush walk* 1957 oil on canvas 92.2 x 73.0 cm
(below) *January 14, 1960* 1960 beeswax, pigments and oil
on canvas 74.5 x 92.2 cm

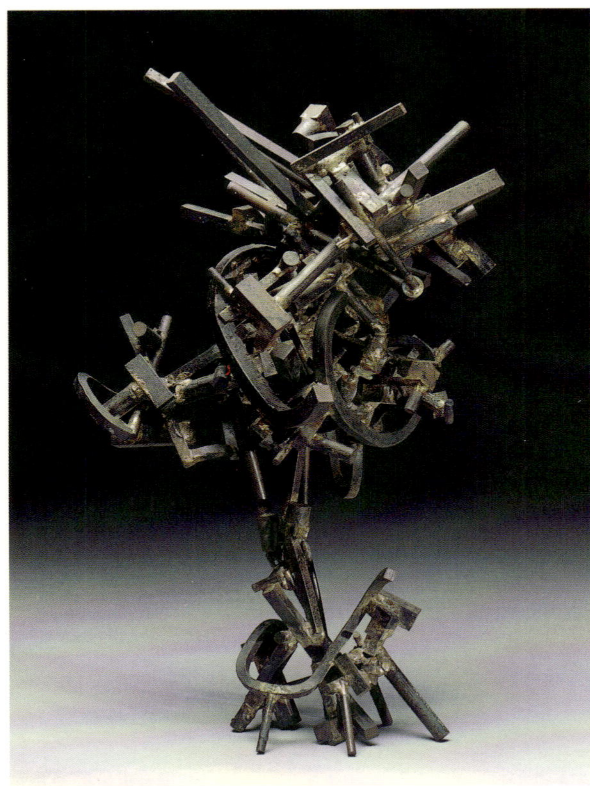

Robert Klippel *Untitled* 1960 brazed and patinated steel
61.2 x 37.3 x 28.0 cm

The group exhibition *Direction 1* at the Macquarie Galleries in 1956 had been something of a watershed for Sydney abstraction, and was read as a challenge to figurative modes of expression. Robert Hughes, in 1966, suggested that the exhibition had 'some claim to be called the most important group show by local painters between 1945 and the Antipodean exhibition in 1959'.[19] Seeing the work of Passmore and his former students Olsen and William Rose, as well as the work of Robert Klippel who had returned to Australia in 1950 after several years studying and working in London, Paris and America, changed the climate for artists experimenting with abstraction in Sydney.

In the early 1950s Klippel was making abstract drawings influenced by European surrealism and concepts of chance. He had spent time at the Abbey Art Centre in England, where he became aware of abstract expressionism through the Scots artist Alan Davie. Klippel's experiments with abstraction in his drawing and sculpture were rigorous and inventive. He ceaselessly explored mechanical and organic forms in his drawing, and commanded a bravura range of styles; the abstract gouaches of 1953–54 move between lightly drawn and flicked passages to fluid, poured and worked surfaces. Klippel spent the years from 1957 to 1963 teaching in Minneapolis and New York, and on his return to Sydney exhibited his welded junk sculptures to acclaim. *Untitled* 1960 is clearly a construction, and a dynamic one, and there are references in the work to cubism, futurism and the Duchamp of *Nude descending a staircase*, which had made a huge impact in America.

Klippel exhibited in group shows in the early 1960s at the Hungry Horse Gallery in Paddington, Sydney. A number of the artists involved in these shows were part of the Victoria Street Group, actively committed to abstraction in art and keen to respond to the Antipodean challenge. This group had formed in 1960 with Olsen, Rose, Hessing and Rapotec, as well as Peter Upward and Clement Meadmore who had left Melbourne after finding the artistic climate stultifying. In 1961, with the addition of Eric Smith, Carl Plate and Hector Gilliland, the Victoria Street Group became '9 Sydney artists', and held an exhibition at David Jones Gallery. Several months later they took the exhibition to Gallery A in Melbourne, making their return challenge to the Antipodeans explicit by arriving in a helicopter brandishing abstract paintings. In her foreword to the Melbourne catalogue for the exhibition, Virginia Spate declared: 'the younger artists are no longer moved by the ideal of a figurative interpretation of the Australian ethos'.[20]

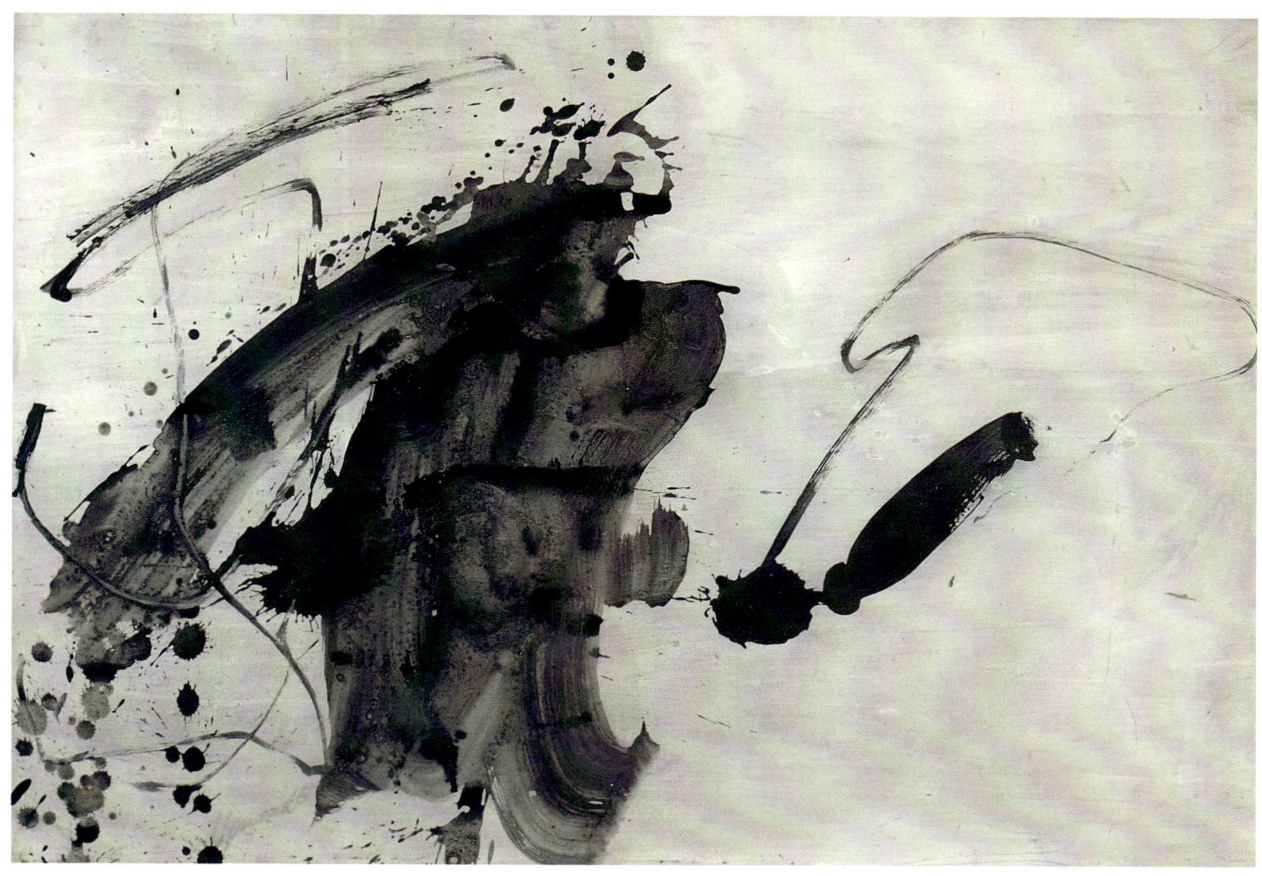

Peter Upward *April drawing No.5* 1961 synthetic polymer paint on paper on board 90.4 x 129.6 cm

Peter Upward was one of a very few Australian artists to fully embrace gestural abstraction. In the '9 Sydney artists' show he exhibited a single painting, *June celebration* 1960,[21] a sequence of calligraphic marks which make up a single gesture across three large panels. Essentially Upward's works are all drawings in paint, and *April drawing N o.5* 1961 relates closely to the larger paintings.

Upward had been influenced by jazz music and the writings of Beat poets, and improvisation was an important component in the making of his work. He was also strongly attracted to the discipline of Zen Buddhism and oriental calligraphy as means to reaching a creative plane beyond that of immediate experience. His paintings and drawings have a kind of controlled spontaneity which registers and images an almost pure life force in the creative act of painting, of coming into being.

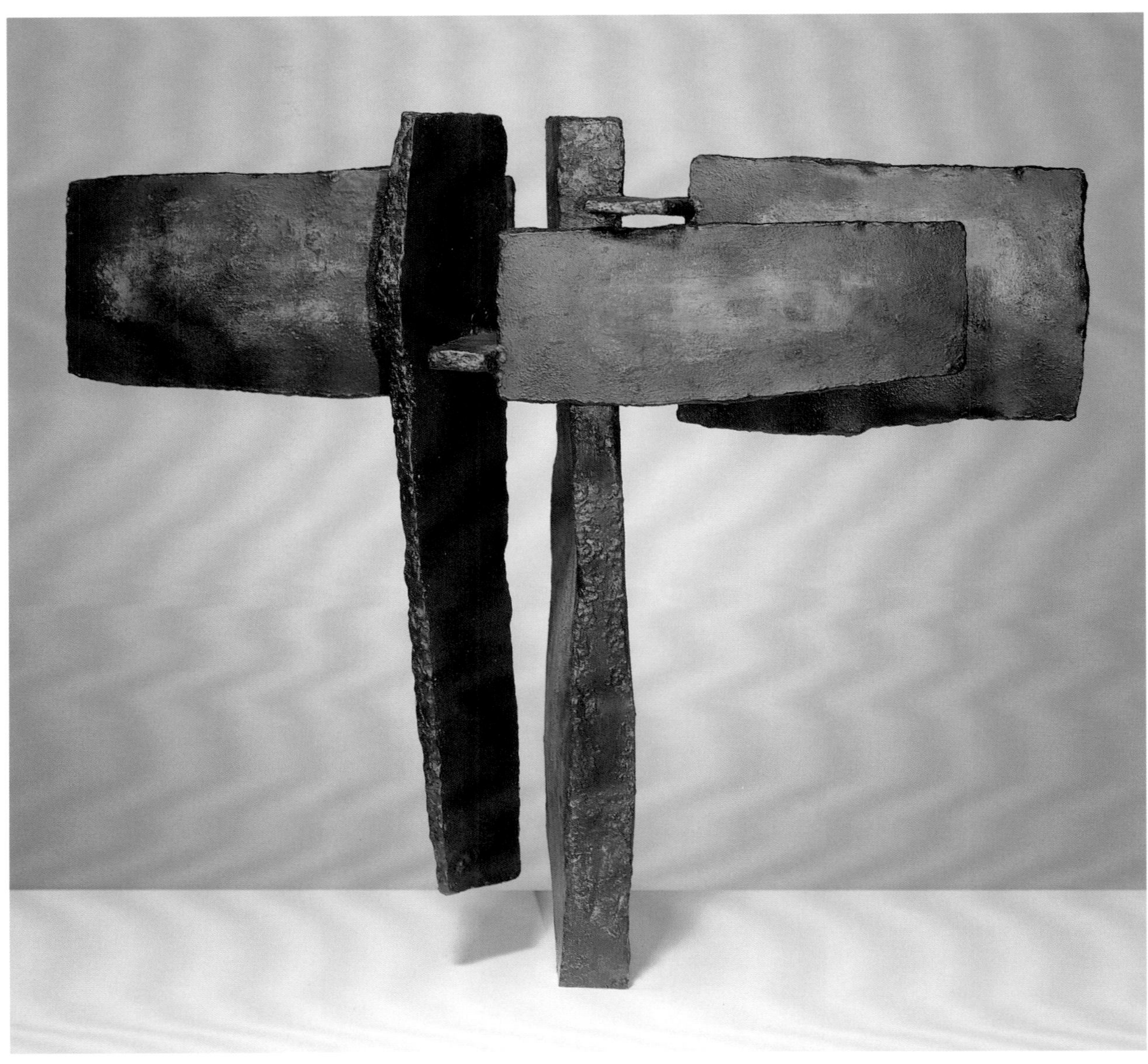

Clement Meadmore *Cross* c.1960–61 welded sheet steel 92.0 x 107.0 x 47.5 cm

Clement Meadmore exhibited four works in the '9 Sydney artists' exhibition including *Cross* c.1960–6, a work which exemplifies his interest in the power of abstract symbolic forms.

Meadmore had studied aeronautical engineering and industrial design in the late 1940s and subsequently he worked as a furniture designer. In 1959 he became the first Director of Gallery A in Melbourne, but left for Sydney the following year. He was making sculptures from the late 1940s and, along with Klippel, he was one of the first artists in Australia to seriously explore the sculptural possibilities of prefabricated metals. Meadmore exploited the inflexibility and potential menace of steel, imparting vitality through burning, scarring and mutilating the surfaces of his sculptures. *Cross* demonstrates his ability to achieve monumentality of form even in a small work. In 1963 he left Australia for New York where he continues to live and work.

Michael Taylor was not one of the '9 Sydney artists', but shared the approach of Upward and Meadmore to art as a symbolic expression of form which carried meaning beyond simply representation. Although his work has had insufficient attention, Taylor must be regarded as one of the few genuine abstract expressionist painters in Australia, and certainly the one with the most sustained commitment to the practice.

Taylor studied at East Sydney Technical College and the National Gallery of Victoria School in the 1950s, and on receipt of a New South Wales Travelling Scholarship in 1960, he went first to Asia, then spent three years in Europe. *Caryatid* 1963 is an example of Taylor's work at its most exuberant. The painting is an expression of restless energy and force. The furling and unfurling tendrils of paint across the surface are part of a complex layering of dark and light tones, which give the work great depth.

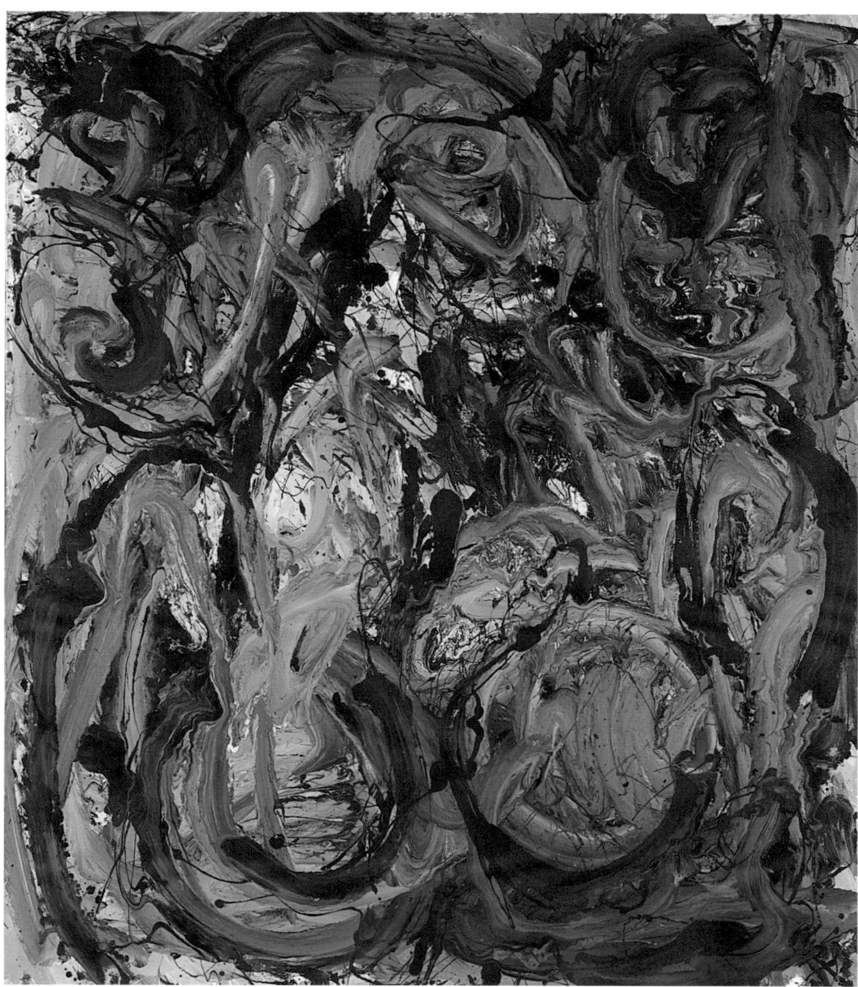

Michael Taylor *Caryatid* 1963 oil, enamel on canvas 198.2 x 170.8 cm

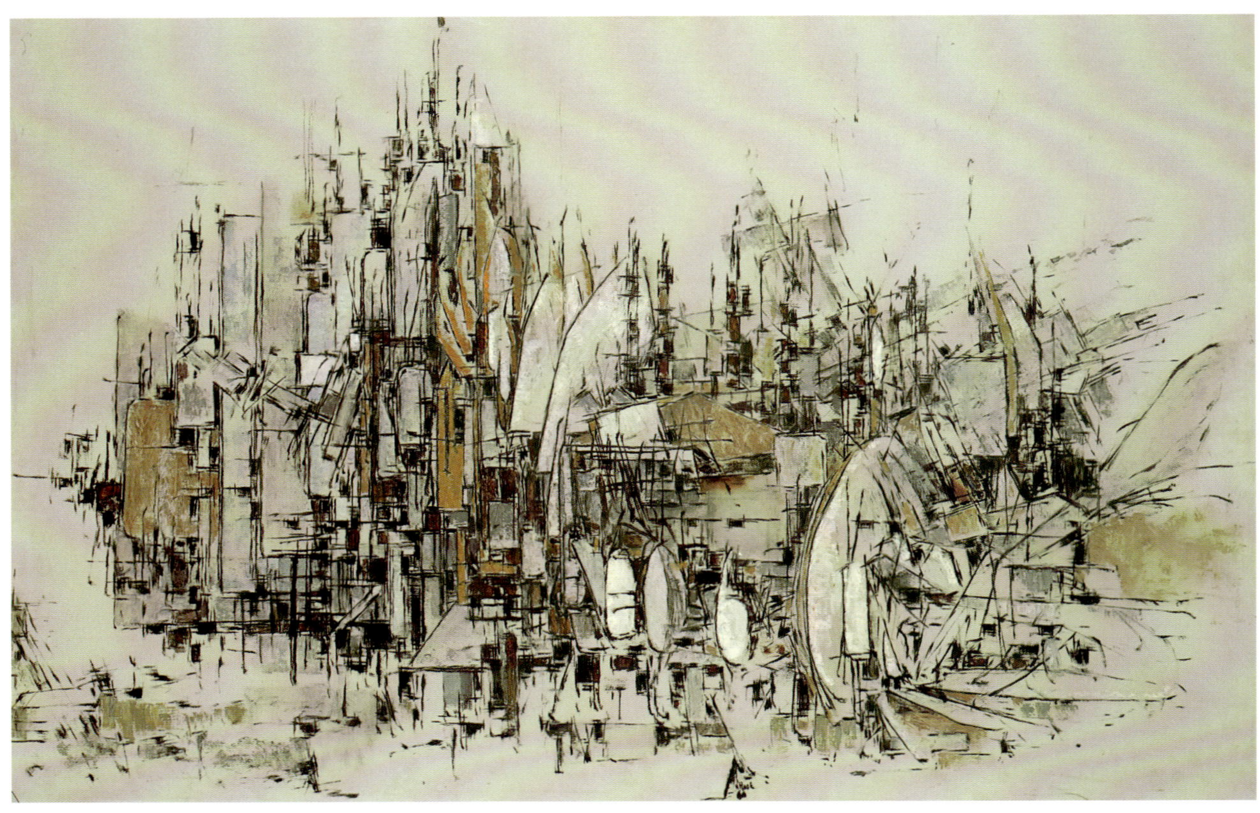

William Rose *Journey into the unknown* 1960 oil on composition board 115.0 x 177.6 cm

Virginia Spate wrote in 1961 that in Sydney 'interest in a more objective, constructed abstractionism seems to have given way to one based in the artist's feeling for the subjective content, the communicable meaning of his conscious and instinctual formal experience'.[22] This was not true for all the '9 Sydney artists' and, in the work of William Rose and Hector Gilliland, cubist and constructivist principles dominated. Elwyn Lynn described the paintings of Gilliland as 'preserv[ing] a cubism in direct descent from Braque and Picasso'.[23]

William Rose's paintings are tightly constructed abstractions which refer to the idea of universal harmonies drawn from the geometry of the universe.

Journey into the unknown 1960 is more fluid and less rigidly architectural than other works by Rose and reflects his enthusiasm for the formal perfection of Mondrian. The dynamic interweaving of curved forms within complex grids appears to make the painting ripple and almost take flight — suddenly it evokes the sails of the Opera House, which in 1960–61 was beginning to take shape. As Geoffrey Dutton noted: 'It was … nicely ironic that at the same time [as the Antipodeans exhibition] the foundations had been laid of Sydney's first great work of expressionist art, which is both abstract and unmistakably an image, the Opera House.'[24]

Carl Plate spent the years from 1935 to 1940 in
America and Europe, and on his return established
the Notanda Gallery in Sydney, where he exhibited his
paintings and sold art books and objets d'art. Notanda
was Sydney's equivalent of Gino Nibbi's Melbourne
bookshop, Leonardo's; both exercised enormous
influence on local audiences hungry for modern art
publications and a focus for discussion. Plate was
twenty years older than Olsen, Meadmore and
Upward; his sister was Margo Lewers, whose
connections with abstract art in Sydney went back to
the Crowley–Fizelle school.[25] Plate's prints from 1959
are quite formal constructions, but in his drawings
and paintings from 1961 a looser element appears.
The heavy forms of *Supporting black* 1963 seem to
be engaged in a slow balancing act whose shifting
rhythms and broken lines suggest seismic shifts.

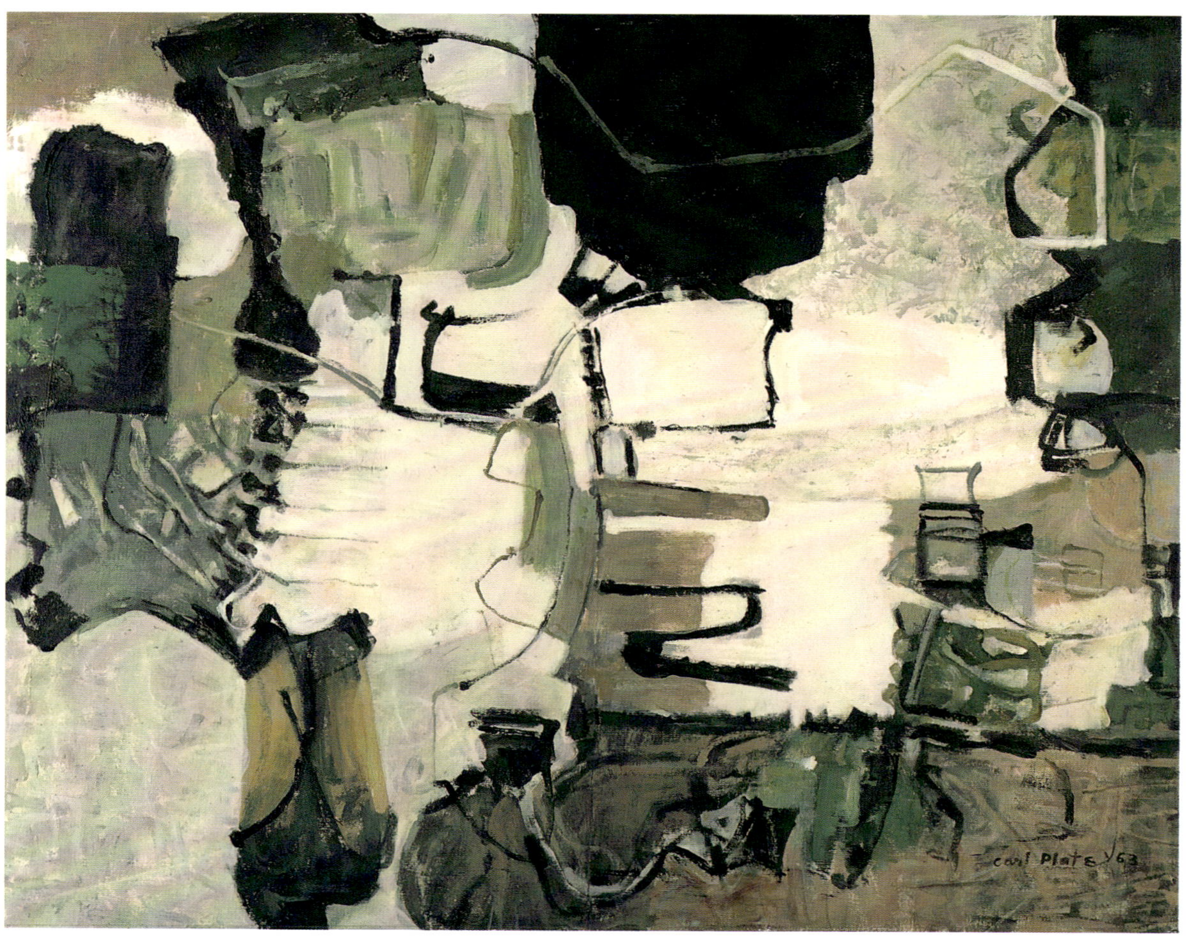

Carl Plate *Supporting black* 1963 synthetic polymer paint on canvas 115.0 x 145.0 cm

There were other individual voices in Sydney abstraction who contributed to the general climate of diversity and experimentation during the 1950s and 60s. John Coburn pursued a style based on formal harmonies of shapes and colours. In his work he invoked an essential human spiritual core, and his imagery was derived from sources as diverse as ancient Mayan and Celtic art. His semi-abstracted designs such as *Tiger Tiger Burning Bright* 1957 celebrate pattern and symbol as distilled representations of the world.

Coburn exhibited at the Hungrey Horse Gallery in the early 1960s and was included in the Whitechapel Art Gallery exhibition in 1961. He won the Blake Prize in 1960, one of a number of recipients during the late 1950s and 60s who succeeded in broadening its traditional Christian base to include more abstract pantheistic elements.

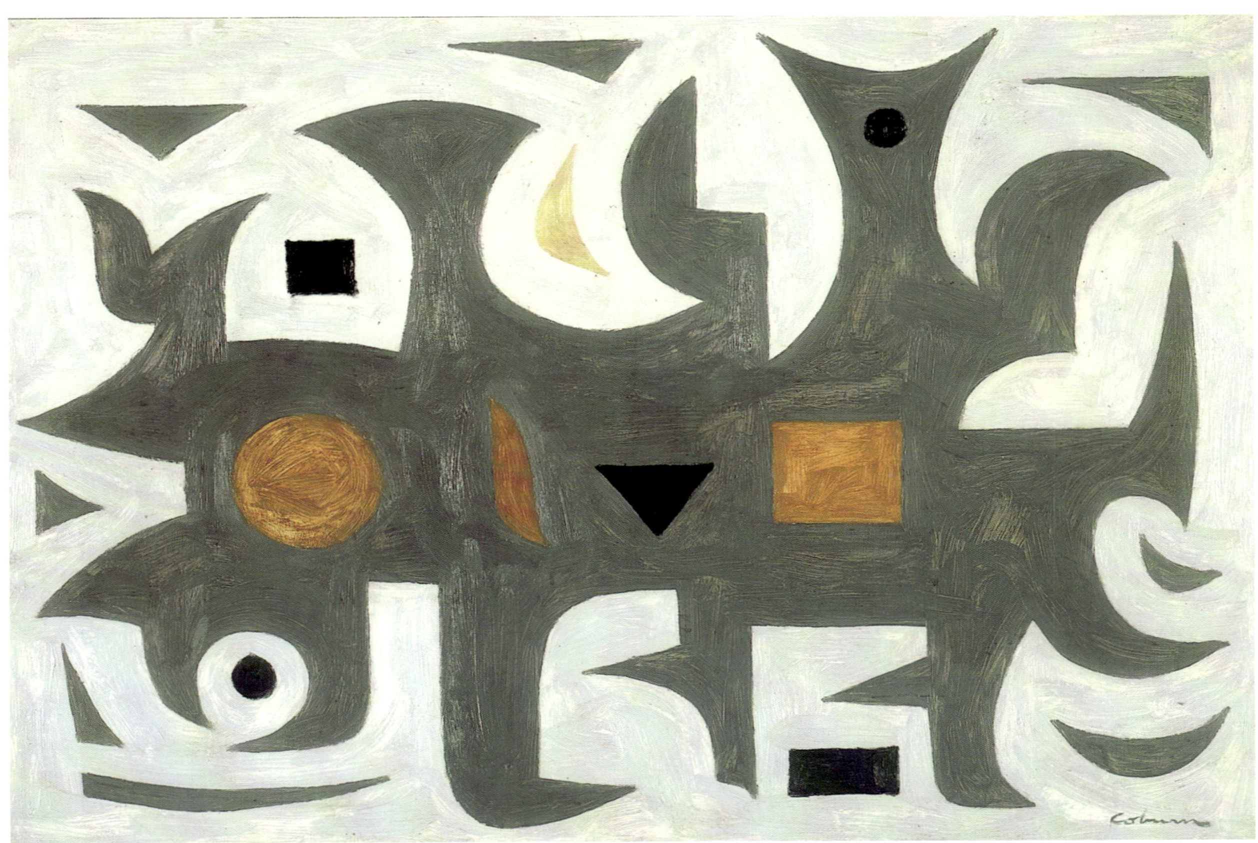

John Coburn *Tiger Tiger Burning Bright* 1957 oil on composition board 60.0 x 89.0 cm Gift of John Coburn 1992

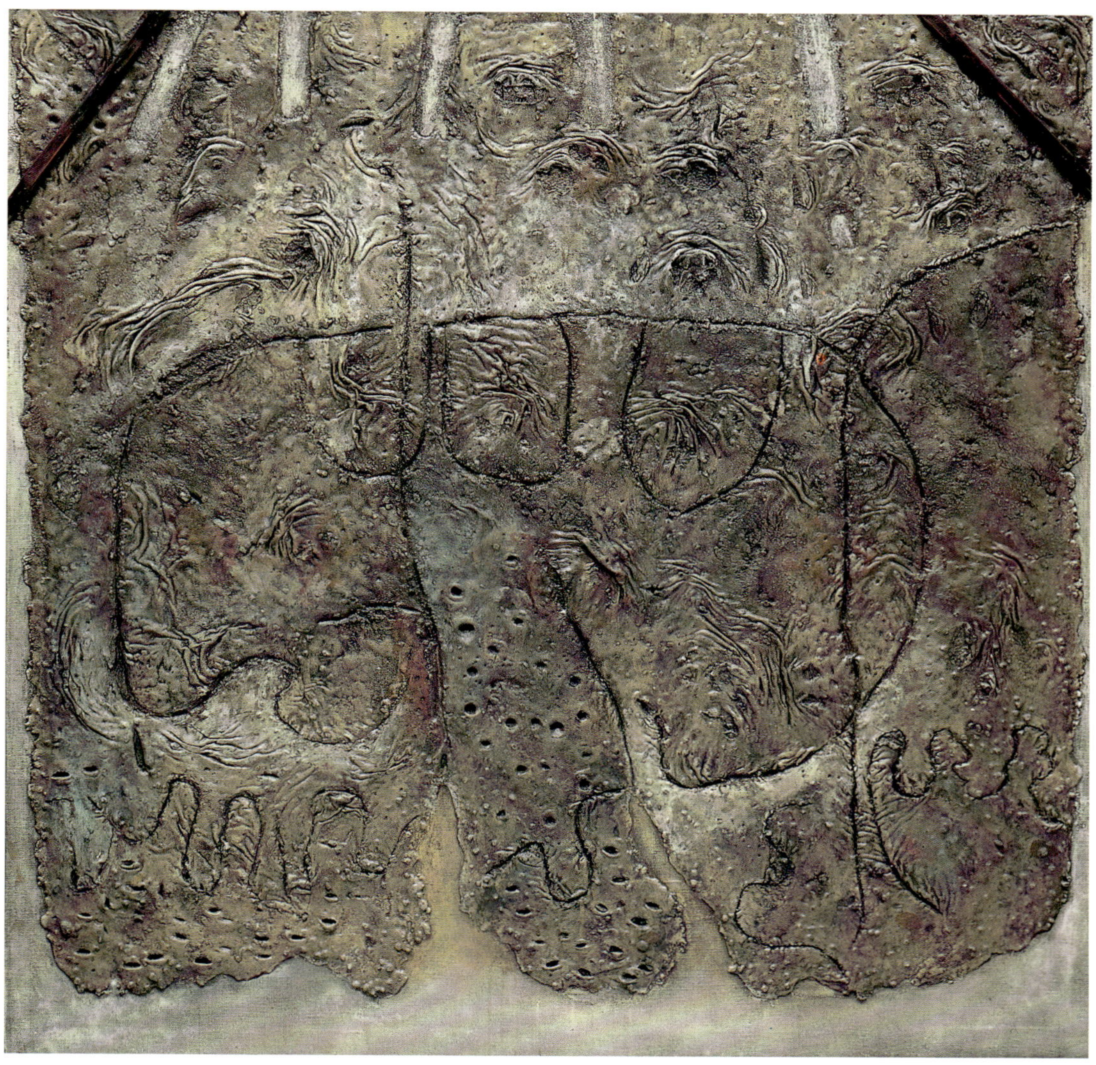

Elwyn Lynn *Hung land* 1966 synthetic polymer paint, sand, wood on canvas 127.4 x 127.4 cm
© Elwyn Lynn, 1966. Reproduced by permission of VISCOPY Ltd, Sydney 1999

Elwyn Lynn began painting in the 1940s, and was influential in Sydney as a writer in the 1950s. He had studied philosophy with John Anderson at the University of Sydney, where he became interested in aesthetic theory. In 1955 he was appointed editor of Sydney's *Contemporary Art Broadsheet* and, over the next few years, wrote informed articles which stimulated critical debate about art in general and abstraction in particular.

Lynn was one of the organisers of the exhibition *Muffled Drums* at Terry Clune Galleries in 1959 — a jokey Dada-inspired response to the Antipodeans which included his own work and the work of Olsen, Coburn and Henry Salkauskas. He travelled in Europe and America in 1958–59 and became influenced by the work of European textural painters such as Alberto Burri and Antoni Tapiès. His previously expressionistic style surrendered to experiments with collage, and he began to embed sand, gauze, rope and wood into the surfaces of his paintings. Images are formed from the totality of the surfaces in a meditative act. *Hung land* 1966 evokes the essential matter of existence through an archaeology of landscape.

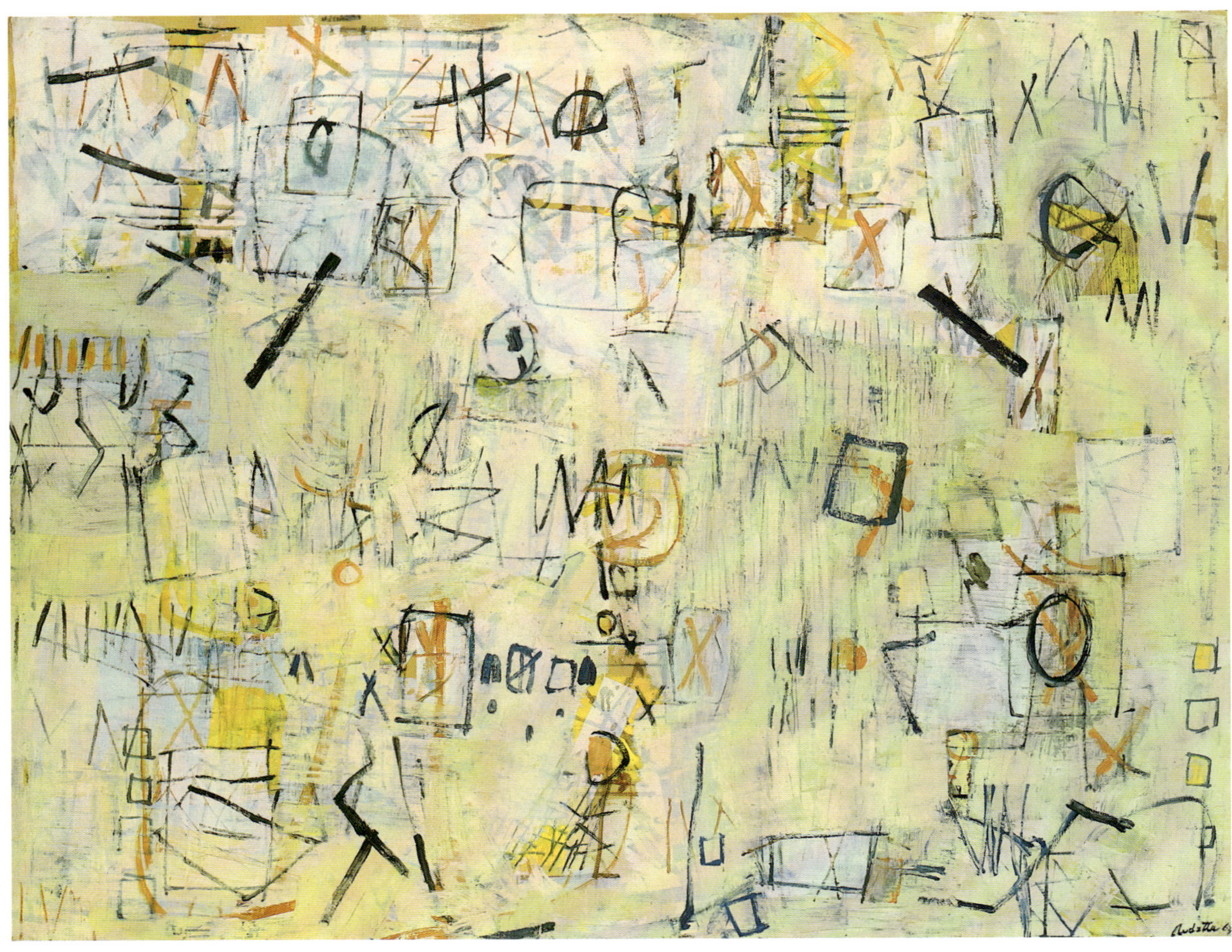

Yvonne Audette *The long walk* 1964 oil on composition board 100.0 x 128.0 cm

Yvonne Audette indirectly but significantly influenced
the development of Australian art in the late 1950s.
During her long sojourn in Europe and America she
maintained links with Australia. She visited Klippel
in New York in 1959, and corresponded with
John Passmore, her former teacher, who stayed
with her in Italy on his travelling scholarship in 1960.
Her abstract paintings of the 1960s such as *The long
walk* 1964 are subtle collections of marks and signs.
They suggest writing and musical notation — systems
which carry meaning through the various elements that
constitute the total work. Julie Ewington has discussed
the influence on Audette's painting of the streets
and the frescoes of Florence, which inspired the chalky
textures and delicate colours that seem to link her work
with that of the American, Mark Tobey.[26]

Tony Tuckson's practice as a painter of gestural abstract works was largely unknown until the 1970s, but his work is now recognised as one of the high achievements of Australian art.

During the 1950s and 60s Tuckson's professional life at the Art Gallery of New South Wales had a significant effect on attitudes towards art, particularly the indigenous art of Australia. Tuckson acquired graveposts and bark paintings from Melville Island and Yirrkala, and organised the first travelling exhibition of Aboriginal art. He recognised that indigenous Australian art was contemporary art, at a time when most museums had consigned it to ethnic collections in the basement.

Tuckson's painting demonstrates just how much he absorbed from his knowledge of contemporary European and American art as well as his engagement with Aboriginal art. His work became more gestural during the 1950s, with transparent layers of paint, overlaid with skeins of marks and calligraphic lines. *Horizontal* and *Vertical*, both of *c.*1959, are fields of intense energy which convey a sense of layered meaning. Tuckson's work is direct and elusive at the same time: in the dense webs and the simple gestures of his painting the interest lies in the attempt to represent what is known rather than what is seen.

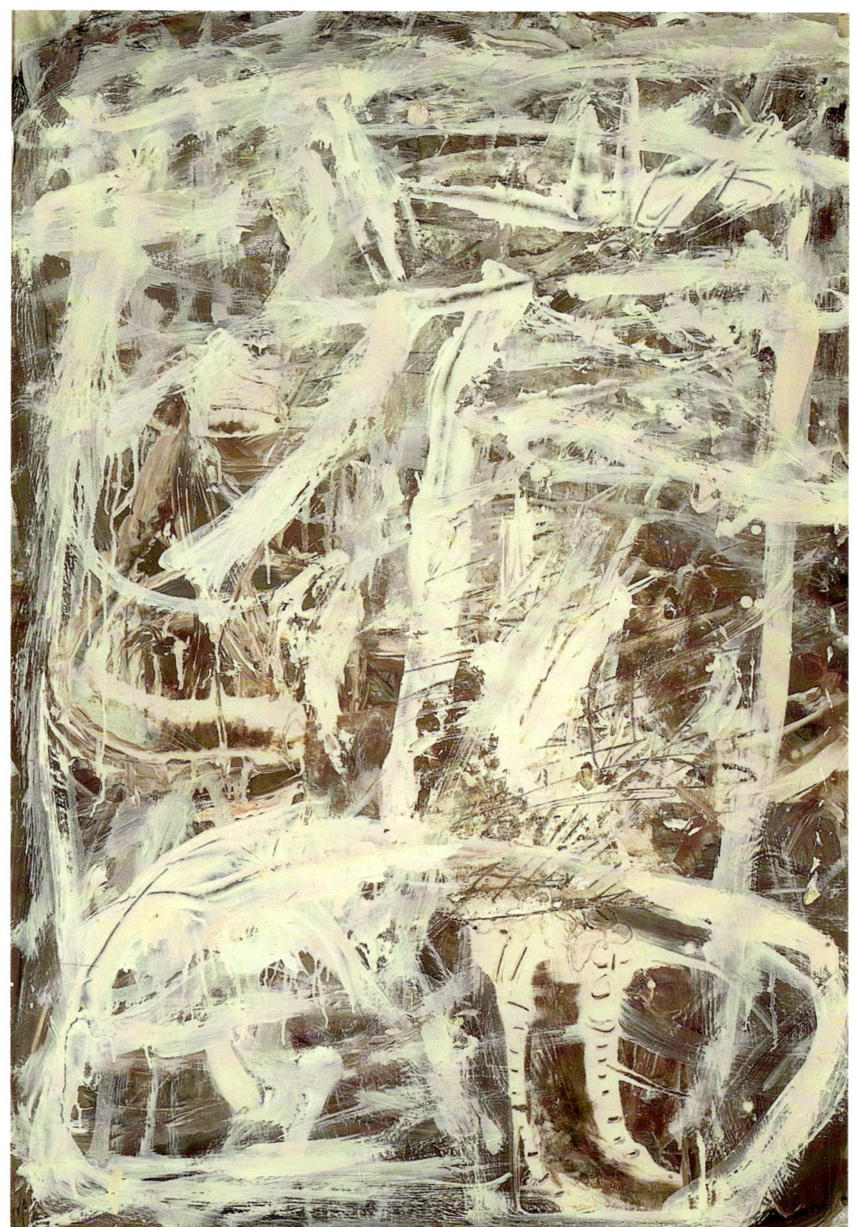

Tony Tuckson *Vertical c.*1959 synthetic polymer paint on composition board © Tony Tuckson, 1959. Reproduced by permission of VISCOPY Ltd, Sydney 1999

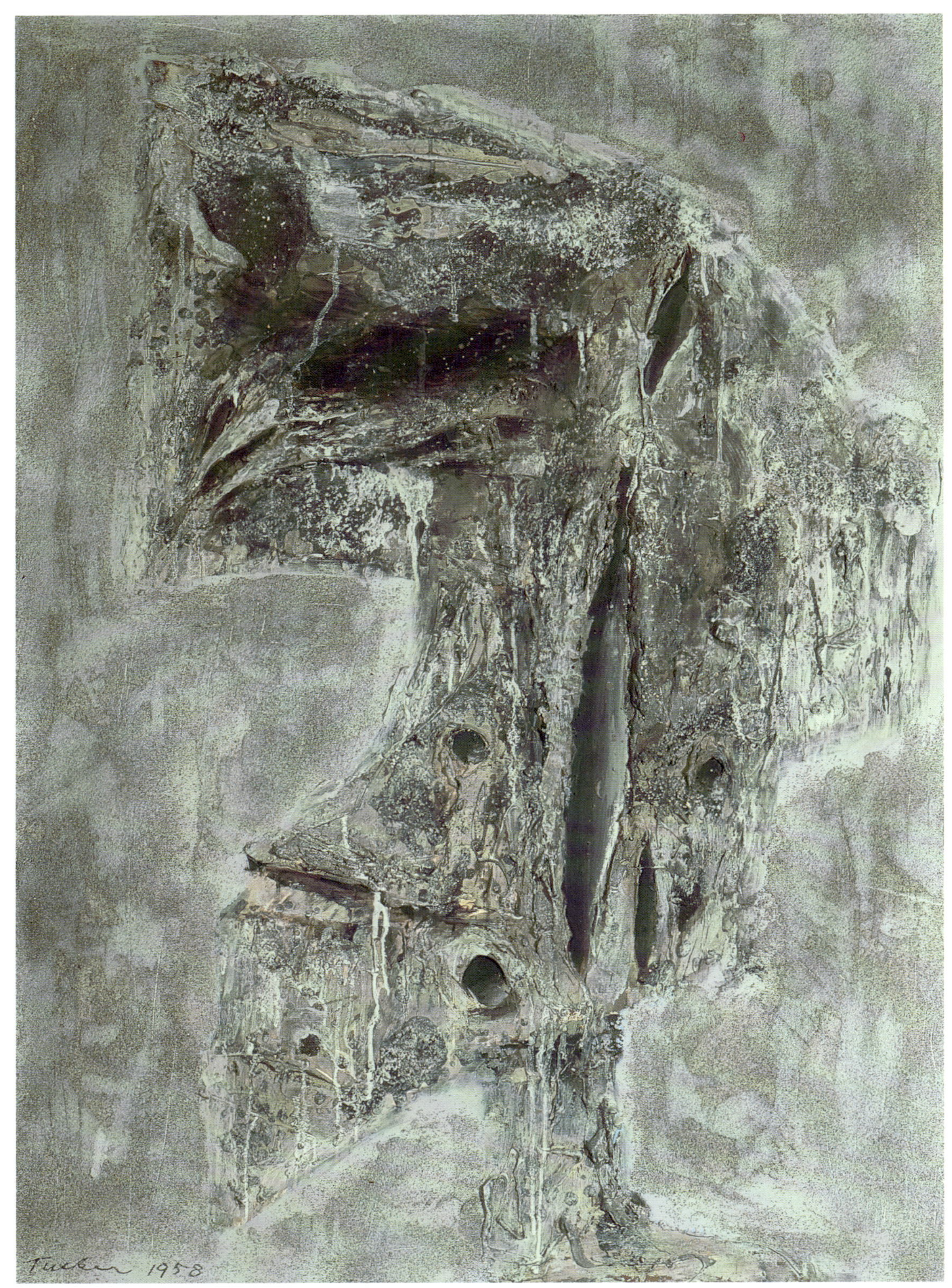

Albert Tucker *Antipodean head* 1958 synthetic polymer paint and sand on composition board 124.5 x 89.5 cm

The decade from the 1950s to the 1960s has been characterised by some art historians as heroic years for Australian art, a time when the tyranny of distance was a positive virtue and local traditions and home-grown mythologies were triumphant. The truth is rather more complex and elusive, and the tensions and conflicts which were alive throughout this period provide much of the creative source for the art being made.

There was no resolution of the figurative/abstract divide, and the clearest symptom of that is the art which falls between two camps, which for many people has come to stand for Australian art of the time — the semi-abstractions of Fred Williams, Leonard French, John Olsen, and, arguably, Sidney Nolan. The fact that this work is so regarded indicates that artists and audiences were becoming increasingly receptive to abstraction. Even those artists who were firmly committed to representation in their work, like Albert Tucker and Brett Whiteley, flirted with abstract modes of painting. When the expatriate Tucker made *Antipodean head* 1958 in London, he was consciously seeking a symbol for an Australian mythology which could still engage with the questions of European modernism, as Nolan's Ned Kelly had done ten years earlier. The encrusted and scabrous surface of *Antipodean head* is directly borrowed from the textural abstract painting of Alberto Burri and Antoni Tapiès.

For artists who vigorously pursued an art beyond national symbols, abstraction suggested the possibilities of an expanded reality. In embracing visual traditions outside European models, and seeking to make art which was essential and not literal, some Australian artists made a crucial link between the developments of modernism in Europe and America and the cultural traditions of the other half of the world, Europe's *Antipodes*.

Deborah Clark

1   Bernard Smith 'The Antipodean Manifesto', in *Antipodeans, 4th – 15th Aug. 1959*, exhibition catalogue, Victorian Artists' Society, Melbourne, 1959.
2   Barbara Blackman, 'The Antipodean Affair', *Art and Australia*, vol.5, no.4, March 1968, pp.607–616.
3   Bernard Smith 'The Antipodean Manifesto', [this author's italics].
4   Some works included in *The Antipodeans: Challenge and response in Australian art 1955–1965* fall outside the period 1955–65, but are included either to give a sense of an artist's development, or as exemplary work by an artist who might not otherwise be represented.
5   See Steve Tonkin's 'In Defence of the Image', in this catalogue pp.6–18.
6   Christine France *New Directions 1952-1962*, Penrith Regional Art Gallery 1991, p.8.
7   ibid.
8   Bernard Smith, *Australian Painting 1788–1970*, Melbourne: Oxford University Press, 1971, p.212.
9   Eleonore Lange *Exhibition 1*, David Jones Gallery, Sydney, August 1939, quoted in Bruce Adams *Ralph Balson: A Retrospective*, Melbourne: Heide Park and Art Gallery, 1989, p.8.
10 Ralph Balson, letter to Daniel Thomas, Art Gallery of NSW, 28 March 1960, quoted in ibid.
11 Such as the 1956 Pacific Loan Exhibition which travelled aboard the S.S. *Orcades* to Auckland, Honolulu, Vancouver and San Francisco, and *Recent Australian Painting* at the Whitechapel Art Gallery, London, in 1961.
12 James Gleeson 'Painting in Australia since 1945', *Art and Australia*, vol.1, no.1, May 1963, p.2.
13 Interview with Ian Fairweather, 30 March 1963, Hazel de Berg Recordings, Oral History Collection, National Library of Australia.
14 Olsen's influence on Passmore has been referred to by a number of writers including Robert Hughes *The Art of Australia*, Melbourne: Penguin, 1970, p.261, and Barry Pearce, *John Passmore 1904–84 Retrospective*, Sydney: Art Gallery of NSW, 1984. Julie Ewington discusses the evidence for Audette's influence on Passmore in her catalogue essay *Yvonne Audette: Abstract Paintings 1950s & 1960s*, Brisbane: Queensland Art Gallery, 1999.
15 Barry Pearce, 'Direction 1', *Art and Australia*, vol.24, no.4, Winter 1987, p.502.
16 For a thorough examination of the impact of European émigrés on Australian art and culture in the period see Roger Butler (ed.) *The Europeans: Emigré artists in Australia 1930 – 1960*, Canberra: National Gallery of Australia, 1997.
17 Robert Hughes, *The Art of Australia*, p 264.
18 James Gleeson, 'Painting in Australia since 1945', p.10.
19 Robert Hughes, *The Art of Australia*, p 264.
20 Virginia Spate, foreword to *Nine Sydney Artists*, Melbourne: Gallery A catalogue number 27, 1961.
21 Peter Upward, *June celebration* 1960, synthetic polymer paint on composition board, 213.5 x 411.5 cm, National Gallery of Australia.
22 Virginia Spate, *Nine Sydney Artists*.
23 Elwyn Lynn 'Avant Garde Painting in Sydney', *Meanjin Quarterly*, vol.20, no.3, September 1961.
24 Geoffrey Dutton *The Innovators*, Melbourne: Macmillan, 1986, p.169.
25 Lewers and Plate were both included in the Pacific Loan Exhibition 1956, and group exhibitions in Sydney such as *Survey 1* at the Blaxland Gallery in 1961; and Plate was represented in the Whitechapel Art Gallery show of *Recent Australian Painting* in London, 1961.
26 Julie Ewington, *Yvonne Audette*, pp.22–23.

THE ANTIPODEAN MANIFESTO

Let it be said in the first place that we have all played a part in that movement which has sought for a better understanding of the work of contemporary artists both here and abroad. Indeed, we are, in no uncertain sense, members of the modern movement in art. We take cognisance of all that has happened in art during the past fifty years — not to do so would be folly.

But today we believe, like many others, that the existence of painting as an independent art is in danger. Today *tachistes*, action painters, geometric abstractionists, abstract expressionists and their innumerable band of camp followers threaten to benumb the intellect and wit of art with their bland and pretentious mysteries. The art which they champion is not an art sufficient for our time, it is not an art for living men. It reveals, it seems to us, a death of the mind and spirit.

And yet wherever we look, New York, Paris, London, San Francisco or Sydney, we see young artists dazzled by the luxurious pageantry and colour of non-figuration. It has become necessary therefore for us to point out, as clearly and as unmistakably as we can, that the great Tachiste Emperor has no clothes — nor has he a body. He is only a blot — a most colourful, elegant and shapely blot.

Modern art has liberated the artist from his bondage to the world of natural appearances, it has not imposed upon him the need to withdraw from life. The widespread desire, as it is claimed, to 'purify' painting has led many artists to claim that they have invented a new language. We see no evidence at all of the emergence of such a new language nor any likelihood of its appearance. Painting for us is more than paint. Certainly the non-figurative arts can express moods and attitudes, but they are not capable of producing a new artistic language. We are not, it seems to us,

witnessing in non-figuration the emergence of an utterly new form of art. We are witnessing yet another attempt by puritan and iconoclast to reduce the living speech of art to the silence of decoration.

Art is, for the artist, his speech, his way of communication. And the image, the recognisable shape, the meaningful symbol, is the basic unit of his language. Lines, shapes and colours though they may be beautiful and expressive are by no means images. For us the image is a figured shape or symbol fashioned by the artist from his perceptions and imaginative experience. It is born of past experience and refers back to past experience — and it communicates. It communicates because it has the capacity to refer to experiences the artist shares with his audience.

Art is willed. No matter how much the artist may draw upon the instinctive and unconscious levels of his experience a work of art remains a purposive act, a humanisation of nature. The artist's purpose achieves vitality and power in his images. Take the great black bull of Lascaux, for example, an old beast and a powerful one, who has watched over the birth of many arts and many mythologies. He is endowed with a vitality which is an emblem of life itself. Destroy the living power of the image and you have humbled and humiliated the artist, have made him a blind and powerless Samson fit only to grind the corn of Philistines.

As Antipodeans we accept the image as representing some form of acceptance of, and involvement in life. For the image has always been concerned with life, whether of the flesh or of the spirit. Art cannot live much longer feeding upon the disillusions of the generation of 1914. Today Dada is as dead as the dodo and it is about time we buried this antique hobby-horse of our fathers.

When we look about us there still seems much to be done in art worth doing. People, their surroundings and the past that made them are still subjects, we should like to point out, worthy of the consideration of the artist. We are not, of course, seeking to create a national style. But we do seek to draw inspiration from our own lives and the lives of those about us. Life here in this country has similarities to life elsewhere and also significant differences. Our experience of this life must be our material. We believe that we have both a right and a duty to draw upon our experience both of society and nature in Australia for the materials of our art. For Europeans this country has always been a primordial and curious land. To the ancients the antipodes was a kind of nether world, to the peoples of the Middle Ages its forms of life were monstrous, and for us, Europeans by heritage (but not by birth) much of this strangeness lingers. It is natural therefore that we should see and experience nature differently in some degree from the artists of the northern hemisphere.

We live in a young society still making its myths. The emergence of myth is a continuous social activity. In the growth and transformation of its myths a society achieves its own sense of identity. In this process the artist may play a creative and liberating role. The ways in which a society images its own feelings and attitudes in myth provides him with one of the deepest sources of art.

Nevertheless our final obligation is neither to place nor nation. So far as we are concerned the society of man is indivisible and we are in it. When we think of all that has happened to people like ourselves during the last fifty years we know that we do not fully understand them – and we want to. How can they bear living? But they do. So we want to ask questions. If such an aim is impure then we would say that purism leads to puritanism, puritanism to image-smashing, and image-smashing, after an Indian summer of decorative luxury, to the death of art.

If the triumph of non-figurative art in the West fills us with concern so, too, does the dominance of socialist realism in the East. Socialist realism, as we understand it, places too many restraints upon the independent creative activity of the artist for it to produce work of vitality and power. We wish to stress that in defending the image we are not seeking to return to naturalistic forms of painting and sculpture but are defending something which is vital to the life of art itself.

We want to say, finally, that we are more directly concerned with our own art, more involved in it, than in anything else. This is not escapism. It is simply a recognition that the first loyalty of an artist is to his art. Today that loyalty requires, beyond all else, the defence of the image.

Charles Blackman, Arthur Boyd, David Boyd, John Brack, Robert Dickerson, John Perceval, Clifton Pugh, Bernard Smith

(*Antipodeans, 4th–15th Aug. 1959*, Melbourne: Victorian Artists' Society, 1959.)

BIBLIOGRAPHY

compiled by Greg Evans

This bibliography is not simply a collection of resources on the
Antipodeans, nor a comprehensive survey of material about the artists
involved in the group. It is a selection that has contributed to an
ongoing discussion on abstract and figurative art in Australia.
Not all citations are annotated and the length of the annotations is
not necessarily indicative of relevance to the discussion. Most items
are held in the National Gallery of Australia Research Library.
Others are located at the National Library of Australia; State Library
of NSW; and the Chifley Library, Australian National University.

MONOGRAPHS

Allen, Traudi, *Clifton Pugh: Patterns of a Lifetime*, Melbourne:
Thomas Nelson, 1981.

— *John Perceval*, Melbourne: Melbourne University Press, 1992.

Beilharz, Peter, *Imagining the Antipodes: Culture, theory, and the visual
in the work of Bernard Smith*, Cambridge, New York: Cambridge
University Press, 1997.
Chapter 4: 'The Antipodean Manifesto', pp.97–126.
The origin, formation and dissolution of the Antipodeans are
detailed. Membership and omissions are suggested as being
coincidental. Letters to Bernard Smith are quoted; John Brack's
resignation; Fred Williams's declining an invitation to join
the group in 1960.
'The Antipodean Manifesto' is reproduced with an accompanying
interpretation of the document. The artists' dissatisfaction with the
Manifesto is outlined.
Subsequent exhibitions and literature on the Antipodeans are
discussed, including the views of Robert Hughes, Barbara Blackman
and Gary Catalano.
The reception of the Whitechapel show in London and the notion
of 'antipodeanism as exotica' are addressed.

Benko, Nancy, *The Art of David Boyd*, Adelaide: Lidums Art Gallery,
1973, pp.9–17.
'The Antipodean Manifesto' is reproduced. David Boyd's conviction
to its claims is discussed. How the other artists distanced themselves
from the document, leaving the responsibility to David Boyd and
Bernard Smith is also raised.

Bonython, Kym, *Modern Australian Painting and Sculpture: A survey
of Australian art from 1950 to 1960*, Adelaide: Griffin Press, 1960.

Catalano, Gary, *The Years of Hope: Australian art and criticism
1959–1968*, Melbourne: Oxford University Press, 1981.
Chapter 3: 'First Loyalties', pp.37–47 discusses the formation
of the Antipodeans, the reception by critics, and analyses the
Manifesto.
Chapter 4: 'Childhood Themes', pp.48–59 suggests similarities
in aims and attitudes between Antipodeans and abstractionists.
Sydney reviews of abstract and figurative painters are evaluated
as equally balanced.
Chapter 5: 'Other Styles, Other Images', pp.60–74 discusses
the noticeable omissions from the Antipodeans group.
'The Antipodean Manifesto' is reproduced in an appendix.

Churcher, Betty, *Molvig: The lost Antipodean*, Melbourne:
Allen Lane, 1984.
Chapter 6: 'The Urban Psyche 1960-62', pp.89–104 discusses
John Molvig's independence and his refusal of an invitation to join
the Antipodeans.

Dickerson, Jennifer, *Robert Dickerson: Against the tide*,
Brisbane: Pandanus Press, 1994.
'Friends and Antipodeans, pp.55–65.

Dutton, Geoffrey, *The Innovators: The Sydney alternatives in the rise
of modern art, literature and ideas*, Melbourne: Macmillan, 1986.
Chapter 10: 'The Sydney Dynamo', pp.137–169.
Dutton suggests that Bernard Smith had misconceptions of the
Sydney critics' attitude to Arthur Boyd's *Love, Marriage and Death
of a Half-caste* series. He believes the professional opposition in
Sydney to Arthur Boyd and other Melbourne artists has been
misinterpreted and exaggerated.

Grishin, Sasha, *The Art of John Brack*, Melbourne: Oxford University
Press, 1990.
Chapter 4: 'The Reluctant Antipodean', pp.55–76 details Brack's
paintings of the period, his role in, and later resignation from
the Antipodeans.

Hart, Deborah, *John Olsen*, Sydney: Craftsman House, 1991.
Chapter 5: 'Resolution in "the siren city of the rat race"
1960–1965', pp.49–82.
Evidently Olsen and others thought 'The Antipodean Manifesto'
'misconstrued' Sydney art and asserted a false polemic.
The *Nine Sydney Artists* exhibition was aimed as a response
to this misrepresentation. Hart considers the boundary between
Melbourne figuration and Sydney abstraction a fallacy. The mutual
admiration between John Olsen and the Melbourne painters
Arthur Boyd, John Perceval and Clifton Pugh is discussed.
Chapter 7: 'Close encounters with the landscape —
"Dunmoochin" 1969–1971', pp.95–110 discusses John Olsen's
move to live near Clifton Pugh and of painting out of doors with
Pugh and Fred Williams.

Heathcote, Christopher, *A Quiet Revolution: The rise of Australian art
1946–1968*, Melbourne: Text Publishing Company, 1995.
A thorough investigation into the Melbourne art scene of the
1950s and 60s

Hughes, Robert, *The Art of Australia* (rev. edn), Melbourne: Penguin,
1970.
See Chapter 9: 'Myths and personae 1947–62', pp.221–250;
Chapter 10: 'Abstract painting 1938–66', pp.251–304.

Macainsh, Noel, *Clifton Pugh*, Melbourne: Georgian House, 1962.

Mathew, Ray, *Charles Blackman*, Melbourne: Georgian House, 1965.

McCaughey, Patrick, *Australian Abstract Art*, Melbourne: Oxford
University Press, 1969.

— *Fred Williams 1927–1982* (rev. edn), North Sydney: Murdoch
Books, 1996.
See 'Williams and the Antipodeans', pp.120–122, and
'Two critical years: 1959–61', pp.122–124.
McCaughey suggests Williams' overseas experience encouraged
him to be more receptive to contemporary trends than most of the
Antipodeans. This may be reflected in his 'non-iconographic'
depiction of the Australian landscape. McCaughey suggests that
Williams felt 'intensely rejected' at his exclusion from the group.

Mollison, James, *A Singular Vision: The art of Fred Williams*,
  Canberra: Australian National Gallery, 1989.
  Chapter 3: 'The early Australian landscapes', pp.35–64.
  Williams was disappointed at not being originally invited to join
  the Antipodeans. However, according to Mollison, his work was
  'inappropriate' for the group.

Philipp, Franz, *Arthur Boyd*, London: Thames and Hudson, 1967.

Plant, Margaret, *John Perceval* (rev. edn), Melbourne: Landsdowne
  Press, 1978.

Pringle, John Douglas, *Australian Painting Today*, London: Thames
  and Hudson, 1963.

Reed, John, *New Painting 1952–62* (The Arts in Australia),
  Melbourne: Longmans, 1963.

Shapcott, Thomas, *The Art of Charles Blackman*, London:
  André Deutsch, 1989.
  'Charles recalls (I) – 1960-6,' pp.2–6; and 'A Life: Part 1',
  pp.7–40. 'The Antipodean Manifesto' is reproduced; discussed is
  the view of the artists, including Blackman, that the exhibition was
  about promotion rather than opposition.

Smith, Bernard, *Australian Painting Today: The John Murtagh Macrossan
  lectures 1961*, St Lucia: University of Queensland Press, 1962.

— *Australian Painting 1788–1960*, Melbourne: Oxford University
  Press, 1962
  Chapter 9: 'Figurative and non-figurative 1950–60', pp.289–332.
  The Antipodeans' defence of the 'image' is presented as the
  culminating episode in Australian painting to 1960.

— *The Antipodean Manifesto: Essays in art and history*. Melbourne:
  Oxford University Press, 1976.
  'The Antipodean Manifesto' is reproduced, pp165–167.

— *The Death of the Artist as Hero: Essays in history and culture*,
  Melbourne: Oxford University Press, 1988.
  Includes 'Notes on Abstract Art' (1983), pp.181–193;
  'The Antipodean Manifesto', pp.194–197; 'The Truth about
  the Antipodeans' (1984), pp.198–213.

— *The Critic as Advocate: Selected essays 1941–1988*, Melbourne:
  Oxford University Press, 1989.
  Includes 'The Antipodeans Exhibition: Notes for the Opening
  Address' (1959), pp.130–134; 'The Antipodean Intervention'
  (1959), pp.135–139; 'The Antipodean Artists' (1959),
  pp.140–147.

— *Noel Counihan: Artist and revolutionary*, Melbourne: Oxford
  University Press, 1993.
  Chapter 19: 'From Moscow to Dead Horse Lane', pp.329–342.
  Smith attributes the Antipodeans' caution towards 'socialist realism'
  as the primary reason for Counihan's exclusion from the group.
  This was despite Perceval's recommendation that he be included.

Smith, Bernard and Smith, Terry, *Australian Painting, 1788–1990*
  (3rd edn), Melbourne: Oxford University Press, 1991.

Spate, Virginia, *John Olsen*, Melbourne: Georgian House, 1963.
  Suggests the influence of the Australian landscape was as equally
  significant for Olsen as contemporary trends from overseas.
  Olsen's art is described as 'national' yet not 'parochial',
  liberated from the conventions of 'preconceived Australian imagery'.

EXHIBITION CATALOGUES

Antipodeans, 4th–15th Aug. 1959, Melbourne:
  Victorian Artists' Society, 1959.
  Includes 'The Antipodean Manifesto' and a list of the works
  exhibited by the artists: Charles Blackman, John Brack, Arthur Boyd,
  David Boyd, Robert Dickerson, John Perceval, and Clifton Pugh.

Allen, Traudi, *The Antipodeans: Another chapter*,
  Melbourne: Lauraine Diggins Fine Arts, 1988.

Clark, Kenneth; Robertson, Bryan; Hughes, Robert, *Recent Australian
  Painting*, London: Whitechapel Art Gallery, June–July, 1961.

Direction 1, Sydney: Macquarie Galleries, 4–10 December 1956.
  The artists involved were John Olsen, Eric Smith, Robert Klippel,
  John Passmore and William Rose.

Dixon, Christine and Smith, Terry, *Aspects of Figurative Painting
  1942–1962: Dreams, fears and desires*, Sydney:
  The Power Institute of Fine Arts, University of Sydney, 1984.

Gleeson, James, (foreword), *Contemporary Australian Paintings:
  Pacific Loan Exhibition on board Orient Line S.S. Orcades*,
  Sydney: National Gallery Society of NSW, 1956.

Grishin, Sasha, *The Boxer Collection: The Sydney Alternative*,
  Nolan Gallery, Lanyon, Canberra: AGPS, 1982.

Guy, John, *The Antipodeans Revisited: Melbourne figurative artists
  of the 1950s*, Melbourne: National Gallery of Victoria, 1976.

Helena Rubinstein Travelling Art Scholarship, Sydney: Art Gallery of
  NSW, August 1958.
  Artists selected were Arthur Boyd, John Brack, John Coburn,
  Wladyslaw Dutkiewicz, Thomas Gleghorn, Frank Hodgkinson
  (winner), Hazel Hughes, Graeme Inson, Jon Molvig, Stanislaus
  Ostoja-Kotkowski, and Clifton Pugh. The Rubinstein Scholarship
  provides a gauge to the recognised artists within contemporary
  Australian art during the years 1958–62.

Helena Rubinstein Travelling Art Scholarship, Sydney: Art Gallery of
  NSW, September 1959.
  Artists selected were Charles Blackman, Arthur Boyd,
  Noel Counihan, Robert Dickerson, Leonard French,
  Thomas Gleghorn, Kenneth Hood, Robert Juniper, Jon Molvig,
  and John Passmore (winner).

Helena Rubinstein Travelling Art Scholarship, Melbourne: National
  Gallery of Victoria, August 1960.
  Artists selected were Charles Blackman (winner), John Brack,
  Leonard Crawford, Robert Dickerson, Leonard French,
  Thomas Gleghorn, Leonard Hessing, Roger Kemp, Jon Molvig,
  William Rose, and Fred Williams.

Helena Rubinstein Travelling Art Scholarship, Sydney: Art Gallery of
  NSW, October 1961.
  Artists selected were John Coburn, Thomas Gleghorn (winner),
  Leonard Hessing, Robert Juniper, Margo Lewers, Jon Molvig,
  John Perceval, Stanislaus Rapotec, William Rose, and Peter Upward.

Helena Rubinstein Travelling Art Scholarship, Sydney: Art Gallery of
  NSW, August 1962.
  Artists selected were John Coburn, Robert Dickerson, Leonard
  Hessing, Daryl Hill, Donald Laycock, Ross Morrow, Clifton Pugh,
  Stanislaus Rapotec, William Rose, and Eric Smith (winner).

New Directions 1952–1962, Penrith: Penrith Regional Art Gallery,
  NSW, 16 August–29 September 1991.

Phipps, Jennifer, *I Had a Dream: Australian art in the 1960s*,
  Melbourne: National Gallery of Victoria, 1997.

Smith, Robert; Thomas, Laurie; Hughes, Robert; *Australian Painting
  Today: A survey of the last ten years*, Brisbane: Queensland Art
  Gallery, 1963.

Spate, Virginia, *Nine Sydney Artists*, Melbourne: Gallery A,
  20 September–13 October 1961.
  John Olsen, William Rose, Stanislaus Rapotec, Leonard Hessing,
  Clement Meadmore, Eric Smith, Peter Upward, Hector Gilliland and
  Carl Plate — the group previously exhibited as *9 Sydney 1961*
  at the David Jones Art Gallery, Sydney, 19–28 July 1961.

Thomas, Daniel; Turnbull, Clive; Young, Elizabeth, *Antipodean Vision: Australian painting — Colonial — Impressionist — Contemporary*, Melbourne: F.W. Cheshire, 1962.
The book was published to accompany the exhibition of Australian painting held at the Tate Gallery in London, January–March 1963.

Zimmer, Jenny, *Abstract Art in Australia*, Melbourne: RMIT Gallery, 1–19 August 1983.
Abstract art in Australia including the Antipodeans reaction against abstraction.

JOURNALS AND NEWSPAPERS

'The Antipodeans', *Modern Art News*, vol.1, no.1, 1959, p.9.
Also on p.4 are letters to the editor concerning the *Antipodeans* exhibition, including one from Clifton Pugh explaining his reasons for joining the group.

'Artbursts-Antipodeans', *Bulletin* (Sydney), 19 August 1959, pp.24–25.

Blackman, Barbara, 'The Antipodean affair', *Art and Australia*, vol.5, no.4, March 1968, pp.607–616. An important account of the Antipodeans, often referred to in the literature on the event.

France, Christine, 'Abstraction in Victoria Street', *Art and Australia*, vol.29, no.4, Winter 1992, pp.468–476. Recollects the arts communities that grew in and around Victoria Street, Sydney, in the 1950s and 60s. Discusses in particular the development of the *Victoria Street Group*, which included the artists Stanislaus Rapotec, John Olsen, Peter Upward, Clement Meadmore, William Rose and Leonard Hessing.

Gleeson, James, 'Painting in Australia since 1945', *Art and Australia*, vol.1, no.1, May 1963, pp.2–19, 48. Gleeson's lengthy article features the development of both figurative and abstract painting. Also in this first issue of the journal is a similar article by Lenton Parr on Australian sculpture since 1945.

Hannan, William, 'A tale of two cities', *Observer* (Sydney), 4 March 1961. Claims that the respective arts communities of Sydney and Melbourne were largely ignorant of each other's activities and the misrepresentation of Australian art resulted.

Haycraft, Deborah, 'The making of a Manifesto', *Art and Australia*, vol.26, no.2, Summer 1988, pp.284–289.

Hughes, Robert, 'Antipodeans go north', *Nation* (Sydney), no. 50, 13 August 1960, p.22. A review of an exhibition held at the Rudy Komon Art Gallery. The term 'Antipodean' is used as a blanket term for the Melbourne artists in the show. Exhibiting artists included Leonard French and Fred Williams.

— 'Abs and figs for export', *Nation* (Sydney), no.131, 2 November 1963, p.18. In this review of the exhibition *Australian Painting Today*, although he praises abstract works considerably more than the figurative, Hughes suggests that the conflict between abstract and figurative has finally eased.

— 'Pugh: harsh, delicate and wild', *Observer* (Sydney), vol.2, no.5, 7 March 1959, p.150. Hughes discusses the art colony at 'Dunmoochin' outside Melbourne, as well as Clifton Pugh's views on non-figurative art.

Lynn, Elwyn, 'Avant garde painting in Sydney', *Meanjin Quarterly*, vol.20, no.3, September 1961, pp.302–306.

— 'Australia rediscovered', *Meanjin Quarterly*, vol.20, no.3, September 1961, pp.337–339. Discusses various London reviews of the exhibition *Recent Australian Painting* held at the Whitechapel Art Gallery.

McCulloch, Alan, 'Battle cry of Antipodeans', *Herald* (Melbourne), 5 August 1959, p.23.

— 'Figurative — or abstract?' *Herald* (Melbourne), 12 August 1959, p.25.

Our Art Critic [Paul Haefliger], 'Exhibition of work by five leading artists', *Sydney Morning Herald*, 4 December 1956, p.2. A review of the *Direction 1* exhibition.

— 'New art movement "arrives" in Australia', *Sydney Morning Herald*, 6 February 1957, p.2.

Pearce, Barry, 'Direction 1', *Art and Australia*, vol.24, no.4, Winter 1987, pp.497–504. A discussion of the *Direction 1* exhibition held at Macquarie Galleries in Sydney in December 1956 and its role in the development of abstraction in Australia.

Philipp, Franz, 'Antipodeans aweigh', *Nation* (Sydney), no.25, 29 August 1959, pp.18–19.

Shore, Arnold, 'Charles Blackman stands alone', *The Age* (Melbourne), 4 August 1959, p.2.

Smith, Bernard, 'A new art group — the Antipodeans', *Contemporary Art Society Broadsheet* (Victoria), no.2, May 1959, pp.5–7.

— 'The London myth about art in Australia', *The Age*, 24 August 1963, p.19. Smith comments on John Douglas Pringle's book, *Australian Painting Today*.

— Framing Fred Williams', *Meanjin Quarterly*, vol.40, October 1981, pp.389–394. Smith takes issue with McCaughey's claims in his book on Fred Williams. Smith recalls the practical reasons that prevented Williams' inclusion in the Antipodeans. Aware that a large group might affect the coherence of its statement, membership was restricted primarily to those present at the first meeting. John Brack and others wished for the inclusion of Williams; Smith thought the artist would not be interested in a group that opposed abstraction.

— 'How to read the Antipodean Manifesto', Speech delivered at the opening of the exhibition *Clifton Pugh and Friends at Dunmoochin*, La Trobe University Art Museum, 1983, *Meridian*, vol.13, no.1, May 1994, pp.61–64. Smith reproduces a letter in which Clifton Pugh declares his belief in 'not nationalistic' but 'geographical' art. The letter encourages the formation of a group to express this. Smith claims that he 'downplayed' Pugh's strong sentiments in the eventual Manifesto. Smith states his belief in abstract art and emphasises that his very misunderstood attack on abstraction was a 'defence of pluralism' and a 'confrontation of aesthetic censorship'.

OTHER RESOURCES

The Hazel de Berg Recordings in the Oral History Collection of the National Library of Australia include an extensive collection of interviews made during the 1960s and 70s with contemporary painters and sculptors.

For interviews with members of the Antipodeans see:
Charles Blackman (1965) DeB107; Arthur Boyd (1965) DeB109; David Boyd (1965) DeB108-9, 111; John Brack (1962) DeB30; John Perceval (1961) DeB14; Clifton Pugh (1965) DeB100; see also Robert Dickerson (1983) TRC1587.

WORKS IN THE EXHIBITION

All works are in the collection of
the National Gallery of Australia,
Canberra, unless otherwise stated.
Measurements are given in
centimetres, height before width
before depth.

PAINTINGS

AUDETTE, Yvonne
Australia born 1930
The long walk 1964
oil on composition board
100.0 x 128.0 cm
1993.7

BALSON, Ralph
England 1890 – Australia 1964
Non-objective painting 1959
enamel on composition board
91.5 x 137.5 cm
1976.737

Matter painting 1960
enamel on composition board
91.3 x 122.2 cm
1969.74

BLACKMAN, Charles
Australia born 1928
Portrait of Barbara 1951
oil on composition board
90.0 x 61.0 cm
Gift of Barbara Blackman 1985
1985.639

Running home 1954
enamel on composition board
91.0 x 121.0 cm
Purchased from the Founding
Donor fund 1985   1985.631

Silence 1959
oil on composition board
121.0 x 91.0 cm
1971.2

BOYD, Arthur
Australia 1920 – 1999
Reflected bride I 1958
oil and tempera
on composition board
122.0 x 90.0 cm
1999.42

BOYD, David
Australia born 1924
Truganini — a dream of childhood
1958–59
oil on composition board
181.5 x 119.5 cm
1962.11

BRACK, John
Australia 1920 – 1999
The girls at school 1959
oil on composition board
81.0 x 61.0 cm
Collection, Elizabeth Summons

The playground (small version)
1959
oil on composition board
76.1 x 68.5 cm
Kerry Stokes Collection, Perth

COBURN, John
Australia born 1925
Tiger Tiger Burning Bright 1957
oil on composition board
60.0 x 89.0 cm
Gift of John Coburn 1992
1992.1422

CROWLEY, Grace
Australia 1890 – 1979
Abstract painting 1952
oil on composition board
61.5 x 87.3 cm
1976.8

Painting 1951
oil on composition board
58.4 x 70.6 cm
1969.194

DAWS, Lawrence
Australia born 1927
The highway c.1956
oil on composition board
91.2 x 137.0 cm
1969.192

DICKERSON, Robert
Australia born 1924
The bank clerk 1959
enamel on composition board
153.0 x 138.0 cm
The Holmes à Court Collection,
Heytesbury

FAIRWEATHER, Ian
Scotland 1891 – Australia 1974
Composition 1961
gouache and synthetic polymer
paint on cardboard mounted on
composition board
69.5 x 70.1 cm
Gift of Lucy Swanton 1981
1981.1828

FRENCH, Leonard
Australia born 1928
In the beginning 1960
enamel, gold paint, synthetic
polymer resin and oil on hessian
on composition board
137.7 x 122.3 cm
From the James Fairfax Collection.
Gift of Bridgestar Pty Ltd 1995
1995.350

GILLILAND, Hector
Australia born 1911
Study of phases 2 and 3 of growth
1960
oil on composition board
68.2 x 91.3 cm
1981.1625

HALPERN, Stacha
Poland 1919 – Australia 1969
Boeuf 1961
oil on cardboard
76.0 x 53.0 cm
1994.247

LEWERS, Margo
Australia 1908 – 1978
West c.1960
oil on composition board
90.0 x 136.5 cm
1964.4

LYNN, Elwyn
Australia 1917 – 1997
Hung land 1966
synthetic polymer paint, sand,
wood on canvas
127.4 x 127.4 cm
1985.1

MILLER, Godfrey
New Zealand 1893 –
Australia 1964
Blue unity 1954–55
oil on canvas
69.8 x 88.2 cm
1969.53

NOLAN, Sidney
Australia 1917 – England 1992
Kelly crossing the bridge 1955
enamel on composition board
91.5 x 71.4 cm
1976.557

OLSEN, John
Australia born 1928
Bicycle boys 1955
oil on canvas
92.5 x 77.2 cm
1969.2

Bush walk 1957
oil on canvas
92.2 x 73.0 cm
1974.325

January 14, 1960 1960
beeswax, pigments and oil
on canvas
74.5 x 92.2 cm
1976.565

PASSMORE, John
Australia 1904 – 1984
Composition c.1957–58
oil on cardboard
50.0 x 37.6 cm
00.157

PERCEVAL, John
Australia born 1923
Black Tasmanian Wattle 1960
oil on canvas
on composition board
83.7 x 91.3 cm
1960.23

PLATE, Carl
Australia 1909 – 1977
Supporting black 1963
synthetic polymer paint on canvas
115.0 x 145.0 cm
1964.9

PUGH, Clifton
Australia 1924 – 1990
A cat in a rabbit-trap 1957
oil on composition board
90.0 x 136.0 cm
1985.1752

*Portrait of an Australian artist
(Kevin Meynell)* 1956
oil on composition board
116.0 x 86.4 cm
1959.168

ROSE, William
Australia 1929 – 1997
Journey into the unknown 1960
oil on composition board
115.0 x 177.6 cm
1963.3

TAYLOR, Michael
Australia born 1933
Caryatid 1963
oil, enamel on canvas
198.2 x 170.8 cm
1972.356

TUCKER, Albert
Australia 1914 – 1999
Antipodean head 1958
synthetic polymer paint
and sand on composition board
124.5 x 89.5 cm
1973.298

TUCKSON, Tony
Egypt 1921 – Australia 1973
Horizontal c.1959
synthetic polymer paint and
collage on composition board
53.0 x 92.5 cm
1974.333

Vertical c.1959
synthetic polymer paint on
composition board
91.5 x 61.0 cm
1974.334

WHITELEY, Brett
Australia 1939 – 1992
Untitled warm painting 1961
oil and collage
on composition board
127.0 x 152.0 cm
1964.5

WILLIAMS, Fred
Australia 1927 – 1982
The half-round pond 1959
oil on composition board
103.2 x 72.0 cm
1972.10

Portrait of Christopher Underhill
1951
oil on composition board
117.4 x 67.0 cm
1971.37

ZUSTERS, Reinis
Latvia born 1918,
Australia from 1950
Pitt Street 1963
synthetic polymer paint
on composition board
122.0 x 61.0 cm
TEMP.9311

DRAWINGS

BLACKMAN, Charles
Australia born 1928
Lovers with floating figure
1953–57
pen and ink on card
10.0 x 12.1 cm
1977.310

Schoolgirl 1953
charcoal on paper
61.0 x 76.0 cm
1977.308

BOYD, Arthur
Australia 1920 – 1999
Aboriginal bride in a truck
c.1951
charcoal on paper
24.3 x 32.6 cm
The Arthur Boyd Gift 1975
1975.3.3126

Embracing figures c.1951
charcoal on paper
38.0 x 18.0 cm
The Arthur Boyd Gift 1975
1975.3.1958

Figure clasping legs of another
c.1952
ink and wash on paper
34.8 x 50.6 cm
The Arthur Boyd Gift 1975
1975.3.2297

BRACK, John
Australia 1920 – 1999
Eating cake 1960
watercolour and gouache
on paper
47.8 x 47.0 cm
1976.28

Two fighting boys 1960
watercolour and ink on paper
46.1 x 57.3 cm
1976.27

DAWSON, Janet
Australia born 1935
Italian landscape drawing 1960
charcoal on paper
100.0 x 70.0 cm
1992.1411

Italian landscape drawing 1960
charcoal on paper
100.0 x 70.0 cm
1992.1412

KLIPPEL, Robert
Australia born 1920
Abstract design 1953
gouache and synthetic polymer
paint on paper
37.9 x 55.6 cm
1976.1255.517

Abstract with white elliptical form
1954
oil, enamel and ink on paper
37.7 x 55.6 cm
1976.1255.537

PERCEVAL, John
Australia born 1923
Weeping angel c.1957
brush and ink on paper
76.7 x 52.1 cm
1977.325.5

UPWARD, Peter
Australia 1932 – 1983
April drawing No.5 1961
synthetic polymer paint
on paper on board
90.4 x 129.6 cm
1986.8

Untitled 1963
synthetic polymer paint on paper
63.4 x 52.0 cm
1976.113

Untitled 1963
synthetic polymer paint on paper
63.8 x 52.0 cm
1989.1544

PRINTS and POSTERS

BLACKMAN, Charles
Australia born 1928
Antipodeans exhibition poster
1959
lithograph
35.6 x 43.1 cm
Gift of James Mollison 1985
1985.1780A

Fleeing schoolgirl 1953
lithograph
26.0 x 20.4 cm
1986.126

DICKERSON, Robert
Australia born 1924
Man with spotted socks c.1978
etching and aquatint
on grey laid paper
29.6 x 22.8 cm
1978.1338

The new dress c.1978
etching and aquatint
30.4 x 23.0 cm
1978.1335

MEADMORE, Clement
Australia born 1929,
United States of America from
1963
Meadmore Sculpture poster 1968
photo offset lithograph
50.0 x 38.0 cm
Gift of James Mollison
00.113

SCULPTURE

KLIPPEL, Robert
Australia born 1920
Untitled 1960
brazed and patinated steel
61.2 x 37.3 x 28.0 cm
1963.49

MEADMORE, Clement
Australia born 1929,
United States of America from
1963
Cross c.1960–61
welded sheet steel
92.0 x 107.0 x 47.5 cm
1962.50

PERCEVAL, John
Australia born 1923
Angel playing a cello 1957
earthenware
height 30.3 cm
1972.529

Fighting angels 1959
earthenware
height 36.7 cm
1976.316